In Pei..
on the Sea

Shipwrecks
of Nova Scotia

Robert C. Parsons

To Dane and Annette. Dec 2000.

Pottersfield Press
Lawrencetown Beach, Nova Scotia, Canada

The Down East Collection #1

Canadian Cataloguing in Publication Data

Parsons. Robert Charles, 1944–
    In peril on the sea
    ISBN 1-895900-32-8
1. Shipwrecks — Nova Scotia — History.   I. Title.
PC2320.S5P37 2000   971.6   COD-950125-8
C525.P37 2000

Book editors: Peggy Amirault, Julia Swan

Cover design: Lesley Choyce

Cover illustration: The wreck of *Atlantic* from *Canadian Illustrated News*, April 7, 1873, courtesy of Special Collections, Killam Library, Dalhousie University.

Pottersfield Press gratefully acknowledges the ongoing support of the Nova Scotia Department of Tourism and Culture, Cultural Affairs Division, as well as The Canada Council for the Arts. We acknowledge the financial support of the Government of Canada through the Book Publishing Industry Development Program for our publishing activities.

Printed and bound in Canada

Pottersfield Press
83 Leslie Road
East Lawrencetown
Nova Scotia, Canada, B2Z 1P8
To order, telephone free of charge 1-800-NIMBUS9 (1-800-646-2879)

Contents

The fishing vessel *Man Alone* being towed near the corner of Regent and Pierce Streets, North Sydney, Nova Scotia, in July 1932. (Photo courtesy Rice Collection, North Sydney Museum)

Author's notes

While researching and writing my previous books of the sea, I had collected many stories of Nova Scotian ships and wrecks that, to me, were unique, fascinating and deserved to be in print. I felt a kinship with the Nova Scotia sea stories of adventure and misadventure — a tie bonded by the common thread of the sea.

With a basic core of stories at my fingertips I then went in search of other accounts — a search that took me to Nova Scotia ports, archives and libraries where I located many other sea tales. With such a vast array of shipping losses occurring along Nova Scotia coasts, it is impossible to relate all stories in this volume. Many remain to be told. Due to space requirements, or because the story had already been adequately written elsewhere, I excluded several significant or especially tragic losses at sea — ships like *Melmerby* (1890), the salt banker *Flora Alberta* (1943), HMCS *Middlesex* (1945), and the trawler *Reliance* (1966). And I wrote little of the victims of August Gales, e.g. *Sadie Knickle* (1926) or *Mahala* (1927). The story of *Flora Alberta*, with the loss of twenty-one men from the Lunenburg area and Newfoundland, was powerfully told in Gregory P. Prichard's book *Collision at Sea* (see Appendix A). Sable Island with its scores of wrecks has a minimal presence here, for that story has been published in Lyall Campbell's book *Sable Island Shipwrecks: Disaster and Survival at the North Atlantic Graveyard.*

I realize several stories in this book are short — too short to really satisfy our need to know more about a particularly poignant mystery of the deep. But if the information had been available, especially where ships disappeared with their crews or where debris-littered shorelines gave the only clue to tragedy, it would have been included.

The stories are presented chronologically within a scope of approximately 100 years, 1873-1970s, and take place on Nova Scotia shores stretching mainly from Cape North to Cape Sable and Yarmouth. However, there are exceptions; for example the steamship *Morien* left Louisbourg for Newfoundland and disappeared somewhere off Newfoundland's shores. Her story is both unique and mysterious. And the wreck of the LaHave schooner *Cashier* with the loss of all crewmen occurred many miles from home.

These stories, all true, yet subject to the vagaries of human memory and the fallibility of newspaper reporting, are supported and cross-referenced where possible by photos, gravestone dates, clippings, diary reports or "first-hand" information coming from interviews and personal recollections told in archival newspapers. *In Peril on the Sea* contains some forty photos and a half dozen illustrations or clippings.

Stories of ships and wrecks inspired many poems, folksongs and hymns, some of which are quoted here. One hymn especially comes to mind — William Whiting's beautiful "Eternal Father, Strong to Save" and the words, "Oh, hear us when we pray to thee, For those in peril on the sea." The book's title comes from those lines and it is to the Eternal Father I give thanks for helping me to produce this work.

Sadly, the ranks of veterans of the sea, those who sailed on the wind- or motor-driven schooners and steamers, are becoming thinner day by day. Their stories of wreck and rescue are becoming fewer. It is to those seamen we owe a debt of gratitude and it is to them I dedicate this volume of sea stories.

Searching for information, learning of the rich seafaring traditions, and writing of the fascinating shipwrecks of the Nova Scotian coast brought me many pleasant hours. My wish is that *In Peril on the Sea* will give you, the reader, as much enjoyment.

Robert C. Parsons
Grand Bank, Newfoundland
June 2000

Acknowledgements

I would like to thank several people for their information or leads to information. Although we usually communicated at long distance, research assistants Kate Currie and Nadine Petrie at the Beaton Institute, University College of Cape Breton, Sydney, were always ready to answer my questions and send material. They led me to Owen Fitzgerald's extensive list of Cape Breton shipwrecks, which in turn gave me incentive to delve even deeper. The staff at the Public Archives of Nova Scotia, Halifax, and those at the A.C. Hunter Library, St. John's, Newfoundland, were very helpful and patient. Captain Harvey Banfield gave me access to his charts of Nova Scotia and the Gulf of St. Lawrence. James Walsh, of the North Sydney Museum, opened the museum after it had closed for the summer and allowed me to browse and to examine material. Alex Hardy and Jack Keeping, friends of mine who also love marine history, were always ready with information and pictures. My in-laws in Dartmouth — Lloyd and Arlene (George) Hillier and family — opened doors for me which I appreciate.

To the Nova Scotian correspondents — especially Les Stoodley of Bridgewater; William Chapman, North Sydney; Willard George, Arichat; Trevor Bebb, Lockeport; Jean Clothier, Tangier; James St. Clair, Mabou; Captain Hubert Hall (Shipsearch Marine), Yarmouth; Wayne Anstey, Halifax; and Sheevaun Nelson, Blue Rocks/Lunenburg — I extend my gratitude for your willing participation and for paving the way to find information I desired.

To the editors who checked my work for historical, geographical, and grammatical accuracy, a sincere thank you.

If errors occur in dates, names, sources, acknowledgements, photo credits or other information notify the author and corrections will be made in any subsequent reprints.

The author may be contacted at:

32 Pearson Place
Grand Bank, Newfoundland, A0E 1W0.
E-mail: robert.parsons2@nf.sympatico.ca

Sources

The listings for sources for the many ships documented here would take several pages, pages that could otherwise be used to relate exciting and disastrous tales of the sea. Thus, as an aid for any subsequent researcher, let it be known that factual documentation of many ships and wrecks comes from selected years of several Nova Scotian papers (*Halifax Chronicle-Herald, Halifax Mail, Halifax Daily Reporter and Times, Sydney Post, Shelburne Gazette, Parrsboro Record, Lunenburg Progress*, and *Liverpool Advance*) and two Newfoundland newspapers the *Evening Telegram* and *Daily News*.

Other sources used were personal conversations and/or written correspondence, Nova Scotian and Newfoundland poems and folksongs, and material that came from "cut and paste" scrapbooks located in provincial archives. The latter often gave the ship's name and her story but not the date or the name of the newspaper. I also consulted shipwreck files kept in various Nova Scotia locations, e.g. Public Archives of Nova Scotia, Halifax.

The author has sources for each wreck or incident that are available upon request.

Chapter 1 (1873)
Great storms, great wrecks

The unwritten code of the sea says if a ship needs help you give it. Sailors and fishermen, realizing all too well the demands and claims of the relentless ocean, believe a rescue favour will someday be returned.

The code of rescue is not only extended to neighbours; Nova Scotians have been offering help to foreign ships and strangers for centuries. Many cemeteries in fishing communities along the coast contain the graves of strangers pulled from the sea by local people.

Atlantic disaster at Prospect

One of the most oft-told sea stories is that of *Titanic* which hit the fateful iceberg off the Grand Banks in 1912. The Nova Scotian cable ship *Mackay-Bennett*, along with the *Minia*, *Montgomery* and *Algerine*, brought 209 bodies to Halifax. Although the *Titanic* epic is well known, it is the wreck of the ocean liner *Atlantic* the people of Prospect have not forgotten. Their ancestors played a major role rescuing survivors and recovering victims.

On April 1, 1873, the large passenger vessel *Atlantic* — owned coincidentally by the White Star Line, the same company that eventually would build *Titanic* — ran out of coal on its westward voyage from Liverpool, England, to New York. Trying to reach Halifax, the great ship sailed too close to shore and ripped its hull open on the jagged rocks. Practically every fishing boat in Prospect rushed to the rescue. Hundreds aboard *Atlantic* died, but the brave people of the small community used their boats to rescue more than 400 people and cared for the survivors until they could get to Halifax.

Atlantic, a 3,700-ton liner built by Harland & Wolfe of Belfast, sailed her first voyage in June of 1871, completing the run from New York to Liverpool in ten days. She had three masts, one funnel and six water-tight bulkheads; indeed, her steering mechanisms, four compound engines and general design made her one of the best liners of her era.

Fitted for the general transatlantic trade, she could accommodate 1,200 passengers, but in April of 1873 carried thirty-three cabin passengers, 794 in steerage and 149 crew. On that April night, 562 were lost including every woman and all children except one. *Atlantic*'s cargo, valued at half a million dollars, was varied — mostly hardware, earthenware, and dry goods, including $25,000 worth of machinery bound for the mills of Fall River, Massachusetts.

Atlantic struck Grampus Reef, about a half mile east of her final resting place, ran along the reefs and ended up on the rocky western shore of Mosher's (or Meagher's) Island. A report of April 4, 1873, describes her lying on her port side, well under water from amidships with the tips of her masts above water. Nearby was a small rock, hardly thirty feet square, and upon this rock 200 or more human beings huddled for two or three hours until rescued by the little boats of Prospect and surrounding towns.

Three of the more courageous of *Atlantic*'s crew decided to swim ashore. Quartermaster George Speakman carried a line with him to Mosher's Island and he was followed by Third Officer Brady and Quartermaster Owens. The three, by means of a line, hauled a heavier hawser ashore, set up a breeches buoy and began transferring people from the ship to shore. Several passengers drowned in the attempt.

In the week after the wreck, scores of curious people came from neighbouring towns: some to watch, several to help divers recover bodies, others to search the shoreline and to grapple the bottom. As divers brought the dead up from *Atlantic*'s steerage compartments, they were taken to Ryan's Island and thence to nearby cemeteries. Several residents were employed making rough board boxes — too crude to be termed coffins — into which bodies were placed. All valuables, money, watches, jew-

Wreck of *Atlantic* on April 1, 1873, as conceived for *Canadian Illustrated News*. More than 200 people stood on the rock, probably shown in the foreground, waiting to reach shore. After the storm subsided, small boats carried the curious, including women and children, to the site sometimes going between the three masts showing above water. Visitors came by sea and land from Halifax, New York and Boston. (Courtesy Special Collections, Killam Library, Dalhousie University)

ellery, letters, were collected by authorities and then the victims were taken away for burial at Lower Prospect, Upper Prospect and Terence Bay. In the old Anglican churchyard in Terence Bay, there now stands a monument with the words: "Near this spot was wrecked the S.S. *Atlantic*, April 1, 1873, when 562 persons perished of whom 277 were interred in this churchyard."

Stories of *Atlantic*'s loss, from the viewpoint of eye witnesses or survivors, have been retold in other publications; thus the tale of one survivor, Michael Carmody, is presented here. Carmody, a native of County Clare, Ireland, and a steerage passenger, was bound for Michigan. Trapped for three hours below deck, he considered his escape miraculous: " . . . About three a.m. I was awakened by a sudden shock of the vessel and immediately leaped out of my berth. The butcher's mate slept in the bunk next to me, and I asked him what was the cause of the shock. He replied that it was the anchor going down, that we were in Halifax harbour. I was sleeping partly dressed. I then went out of my bunk and saw a crowd of people rushing up the gangway. I asked them what was the matter, and was told that the ship was sinking and she was then half full of water. I turned to go back to my bunk for my boots and hat when a sudden lurch of the vessel threw me with much force against the opposite side of the steerage cabin."

Carmody then tried to get out to the deck, but could not for the immense volume and force of water rushing into the steerage area. Indeed the impact of water threw him up against the bulwarks and kept him under water for a minute or so.

He remembered: " . . . I caught hold of an iron stanchion (crossbeam) by which means I was able to keep clear of the rushing water. While I was still holding, a wave swept me from the lee side to the starboard side and threw me across one of the upper tier of bunks, in which position I remained for about ten minutes. Another wave came and smashed the bunk on which I reclined to pieces, and threw me back again into the seething waters.

"At this time there were hundreds of passengers drowning all around me. I succeeded a second time in catching hold of another stanchion, which saved me from drowning for I had given up all hopes. In this position, still clinging with a grip of despair, I remained for nearly two hours my body swinging to and fro with the action of the water. Sometimes I got a rest for my feet when the dead bodies of the drowned passengers which were floating all round would roll in a heap under my feet."

Swinging from a crossbeam, feet in the water, twenty or thirty feet of water below him, Carmody survived by the sheer strength of his arms. He knew he could not hold on much longer when he heard " . . . voices over my head, as of people talking, and I shouted, 'For God's sake, help me up out of this.' Another passenger, a Welshman, who was above me, hearing me call for assistance, reached down and catching me by the shirt, pulled me up to where he and two others were endeavouring to break the porthole window. We succeeded in doing this, and assisted each other in getting out through the porthole and on to the starboard side of the ship which was above water.

"When we got on the side of the ship to my great joy I perceived land about fifty yards off. About one half the passengers who were saved were standing on a rock. I remained about an hour on the side of the vessel almost exhausted. Becoming numbed with the cold and my strength rapidly failing, I determined to make an effort to reach the lines where the passengers were being rescued. This I succeeded in doing and landed safe on the rock. I had lost the use of my feet by this time and could not stand."

About 200 people clustered on this rock. One can only imagine their abject terror not knowing when the seas would sweep them off, or if any help would come. Bodies of drowned passengers, some of whom were friends and relatives, washed back and forth in the surf around the boat and rocks. Carmody lay there for two more hours; then miraculously the little boats from Nova Scotia appeared.

The Irishman recalled: "I remained on the rock until the boats came to take the passengers off, and was obliged to pitch myself head-first into the boat, as I could not move my feet. After I was taken to the mainland, I was carried to the nearest house, Mr. Clancy of Prospect, where I was put in bed and kindly attended to until the steamer came after us next day and brought us to Halifax."

The only child to be rescued, John Hudley of Lancashire, England, was in his bunk asleep when he (as he reported later) heard a loud crash and a great commotion. He got up, followed some men through a window leading to the deck, and there took a firm grip on the rigging and held on until rescued.

Six lifeboats were freed from the davits; some were swept away before anyone could get in, others capsized as soon as they were launched, and the last one stayed afloat for a few minutes before it rolled, dumping its passengers into the sea.

Captain James Agnew Williams, who survived the wreck, was heard to remark that he would have given his life if only one woman had survived. According to stories circulating later, men pushed their way into lifeboats ahead of women and forced themselves into the breeches buoy first. Husbands left wives and children on the open deck to be swept away, while they saved themselves by jumping into the rigging.

The Clancy family of Prospect, like scores of others, cared for, sheltered, fed, and clothed survivors who, like Michael Carmody, knew no one in the land and had lost what meagre worldly goods they once possessed. The gratitude of survivors could only be expressed in words and they found every opportunity to do so. An American, who was a cabin passenger aboard *Atlantic*, said, "I think I should like to live in a country whose people high and low, rich and poor, are so kind as I have found the Nova Scotians. While I live I shall especially remember with gratitude the kindness of those fisherman families at Prospect." (Appendix B lists some of those families.)

On April 4, 1873 the Halifax *Daily Reporter* detailed the gruesome task of recovering and burying victims of the *Atlantic* shipwreck, which grounded near Prospect three days previously.

August Gales

In late summer, hurricanes originating near the Tropic of Cancer lash their way northward devastating parts of the Caribbean and southern United States. By the time these violent winds reach the Maritimes much of their fury is spent, but the final flick of a hurricane's tail across the fishing grounds and into exposed harbours comes suddenly and with deadly results for schooners. Locally, these wind storms were called the August or September Gales.

On Sunday, August 24, 1873, there occurred a tremendous storm that lingered long in the memories of those who experienced it. The Sunday morning started well; at North Sydney the weather was "dull and heavy," but by noon heavy rain began, driven by a southeast wind that changed to gale force in the early evening and by midnight roared into a raging hurricane.

"A gloomier and wilder night no one can imagine," a North Sydney *Herald* reporter wrote. "Vessels riding over the best mooring ground in the harbour were rapidly drifting ashore, dragging great anchors weighing 2,000 pounds . . . The howl of the storm drowned the loud cries of the shipwrecked sailors scrambling up the cliffs or in terror clinging to the rigging. Monday morning presented a gloomy spectacle. A barque's mainmast here, a schooner's foremast there, booms, bowsprits, mainsails, staysails, mixed up with what was once running and standing rigging."

Throughout Sunday night and Monday morning, towns along the Atlantic shore of Nova Scotia and Cape Breton suffered tremendous damage to shipping and a death toll of scores. The Glace Bay area took the brunt of the gale and in that brief time ten barques, twenty-nine schooners, two brigs, and seven brigantines were destroyed. *Wave*, a schooner owned by A. Hart of Canso, went down at Petit-de-Grat when she dragged her anchors and went to pieces. All of her crew perished. An American schooner, while attempting to enter Petit-de-Grat on the western shore, struck a reef near Black Point and went down. The fishing schooner *Thetis*, out of LaHave, wrecked on the north side of Prince Edward Island; all twelve crewmen, including Captain Corkum, his two brothers, and three brothers named Shenkel drowned.

Generally the August Gales were localized and intense, thus some harbours and areas were not hit as hard as others. No ships were reported wrecked in Halifax where the winds were not as violent. Yet off Louisbourg, *Carrie Douglas*, a 172-ton schooner out of Sydney, went down. *Amy Carter*, a 60-ton schooner owned in Halifax, left Halifax for Newfoundland but went ashore at Liscomb, Nova Scotia.

The toll in ships on North Sydney beach was great: a 55-ton schooner *Mary and Charles*, from Saint John, New Brunswick, was wrecked. So were two ships from Halifax (*Maggie*, a 118-ton schooner, and *John Gilpin*) and two brigantines from St. John's, Newfoundland — *Volant*, at 242 tons and the 130-ton *Hunter*. Commanded by Captain Martin and loaded with lumber ready to leave port, *John Gilpin* lost her jib boom, bowsprit, rudder, bulwarks, and part of her deck load when she collided with the brigantine *Georgina*. Others were luckier and received damage that could be repaired.

The Lunenburg schooner *Union* was lost on the west side of Port Hood harbour. *Bonnie Jean*, a brig from Shelburne, was found ashore on Cavendish sands, PEI, totally wrecked with all hands lost. Another Nova Scotian vessel reported lost with thirteen crewmen on the Newfoundland coast was *Young Nova Scotian* out of Vogler's Cove. The largest vessel wrecked was the steamer *Saltwell*, over 1,000 tons and registered in Newcastle, New Brunswick. She was lost on Scaterie Island and six men went down with her. *Peter and John*, a ship out of Port Hawksbury and netting 216 tons, broke up at Cape Arichat while the Arichat schooner *Samuel Jones* was wrecked at Cheticamp.

Many towns did not have a large number of ships destroyed but suffered great loss of life. An example is Arichat, located on Cape Breton's southeastern shore. Commanded by Captain Jeffrey Boudrot the brig *Ellen*, a 122-ton vessel owned in Arichat, was wrecked in Caribou Cove, Strait of Canso. None of the crew survived.

A week after the storm two divers, John Defries and Michael Lynch, investigated the wreck of *Ellen*. They found the brigantine in nine fathoms of water, lying on an even keel with the foremast broken off under the top and the mainsail single reefed. All that remained where the lifeboat had been stationed was the boat's mooring line. The crew's sea chests were secured with rope, as if ready to put in a lifeboat. Divers could not see anything forward of the fore hatch. The hatch cover was off and the ship's rigging, as well as several fishing nets, was tangled about the *Ellen*'s bow. Her cargo of Sydney coal could not be salvaged.

More disturbing were the four bodies found in the cabin, two men and two boys. The boys were lying down, both on their backs. The two men were standing — one with his arm raised as if in the act of grabbing something to help himself up. The bodies recovered were Paul Goyetchis and his son, a man named Fougere, and Captain Boudrot's 7-year-old son. Still missing were the bodies of the captain, two other crewmen, and James Grath, presumably a passenger. One item recovered from the cabin by the divers was a valise in which were papers and a letter addressed to Grath. Apparently, from the papers dated 1870 and 1871, he once lived in or near Bear Cove, Digby County.

Another footnote to this tale of destruction involves the house of Goyetchis; during the gale his home, along with others, had blown down and the contents scattered throughout the area. The fishermen of Arichat suffered devastating setbacks for many lost their sheds and stores containing the season's dried fish and the townspeople certainly faced destitution in the coming winter.

But the wreck of *Ellen* was not the only sea loss in Arichat. Up to September 13, the schooner *Ann* had not turned up in any port and was declared lost with her crew. She was bound from Sydney with coal to

Halifax and was last seen off Devil's Island on the evening of the great storm. Other vessels saw *Ann*'s five crewmen on deck constantly working at the pumps. She was an old vessel and many felt with certainty she had foundered. Her captain, Grimes, left a wife and a family of seven or eight children — the oldest was twelve.

Further south at Liverpool, in Queens County, came the news of a disastrous shipwreck of the schooner *Tyro*, owned in nearby Brooklyn. *Tyro*'s crew of twelve perished in the wreck off Old Harry Head, Magdalen Islands. Residents saw the vessel go down and debris floated ashore, including the name board with "Tyro" painted on it. Her crew — mostly married men with families from the Liverpool–Brooklyn area — was identified as Spencer Smith and his three sons, Nathaniel, Josiah and Spencer, Hiram Godfrey, William Doutor, Henry Horne, John A. Mouser, William Mouser, Jr., Joseph Wentzell, James Pentz, and a man named Jones.

After a day of destruction and death the horrific storm quickly blew itself out. More than sixty ships were gone. Twenty years previously, in 1853, forty large vessels were destroyed along the coast of Cape Breton during a hurricane, but the August Gale of 1873 surpassed even this tremendous toll. The tales of that day, passed down by word of mouth and written, became legend.

Seamen from other countries who were off Nova Scotia during the storm and survived never forgot the experience. A case in point is Samuel Harris of Grand Bank, Newfoundland. Many years after the storm, he wrote a brief note about it in his personal diary. At the age of 23, Harris had command of his first vessel, *Jennie S. Foote*, and was making his first voyage across the Gulf of St. Lawrence. In his memoirs, dated August 24, 1923, Harris wrote of his death-defying experience: "Today is the 50th anniversary of the great gale of August 24, 1873, which swept the Nova Scotia coast and carried scores to a watery grave. I was off Canso on my way to Sheet Harbour in the schooner *Jennie S. Foote*, my first year master."

The fall of the year is always a time of hurricanes and great wind storms. In an earlier era, without the benefit of long-range weather forecasting and rapid electronic communication, schooners and those who manned them fell easy prey to the unannounced arrivals.

Chapter 2 (1892–1903)
"No hope for either crew"

It is a rare occurrence in these times for a modern ship fully equipped with up-to-date navigational aids to disappear during a sea voyage. But in the era of sail and steam, especially before 1900, disappearances were more common. There were no telephones, few radios and telegraphy was in its infancy. When a sailing vessel was battered by ocean storms, the crew had to battle the elements without being able to notify a port or another vessel of impending disaster.

Many of the early Nova Scotian ships wrecked or lost were banking schooners, so named because they worked the fishing banks off Nova Scotia and Newfoundland. During exceptionally stormy weather conditions, it was not uncommon for these sail-powered vessels while fishing far from port to be overwhelmed. Several disappeared with the loss of all hands without any word of exactly what happened. Owners, relatives and loved ones remained in anxiety and distress for weeks and months until hope was finally abandoned.

LaHave schooner *Cashier*: a fatal collision

So it was with ships like *Cashier*, a schooner which sailed out of La-Have in 1892. An ocean storm claimed her with no survivors to tell the tale. Yet, there was one man who saw *Cashier* in her final hours. Several years ago Clyde Forsey, an elderly gentleman of Grand Bank, Newfoundland, told me how his father James, the master of the fishing vessel *Mary F. Harris*, survived a killer storm on the fishing banks. Two other schooners, one a Nova Scotian banker, anchored near the *Harris* were lost.

During the tail end of a hurricane, which lashed the south coast of Newfoundland and the offshore banks in 1892 (later referred to as the August Gale of 1892), three fishing schooners were lying to in close proximity on the Grand Banks: Captain Alfred Reinhardt's Nova Scotia schooner *Cashier*, and two banking schooners from Grand Bank, the 71-ton *Mary F. Harris* captained by James Forsey, and the 78-ton *George Foote*. The latter was a 72-foot vessel built six years before at Grand Bank and commanded by Captain Sam Patten.

A knowledge of weather lore gathered from years on the high seas led all three captains to believe that an intense gale was pending. As the wind rose to gale force, each captain knew it was useless to attempt to sail for some sheltered harbour. Time was short. Knowing their only recourse was to ride out the storm, they anchored their schooners on the banks and battened down to weather out a gale with winds, at times, of hurricane force.

That night, braving the high winds and mountainous waves, a worried James Forsey carefully made his way to the bow of *Mary F. Harris*, holding tightly to lifelines to keep from being swept overboard. Seas and wind ripping over the deck forced him to grip the safety ropes as he sat on the windlass to check the straining anchor chain. Unable to use his hands, he slipped off one boot and felt for vibrations on the cable or chain with his foot. Movement and play would indicate if the anchor dragged or held firm. Should it drag, the vessel would be at the mercy of the wind and could easily capsize or collide with another schooner bringing death to all on board. Carefully nursed throughout the gale, *Mary F. Harris* stayed afloat through that long night.

After checking his own vessel Captain Forsey noted, as he peered through the spray, that the riding lights of one of the other vessels had disappeared. He was unable to identify which schooner, nor could he determine if it had capsized or been driven away by the wind.

At daybreak he found the answer. *Cashier*, still lying at anchor, was partly submerged, waterlogged and swaying helplessly before the wind with no sign of life. The other schooner, *George Foote*, from his home town and with seventeen men — many of whom he knew well — was nowhere in sight. One fisherman on *George Foote* was Leonard Hartling, aged 40 and born in Liscomb, Nova Scotia, who was married to Mary Patten of Grand Bank. They had a child, Almira.

When wind and sea abated, Forsey and seaman John Nichole rowed to the derelict hull, climbed aboard, but saw no one. Fearing the worst, Forsey then searched the area for some indication of what had happened to the *George Foote* and to the crew of the partially submerged *Cashier*. If the *Cashier's* crew had taken to lifeboats or the dories, they wouldn't last long in the high seas. Later he discovered buoys, trawl tubs, broken dories, and other floating debris clearly marked as belonging to *George Foote*. This evidence led Forsey to believe both vessels had dragged their anchors during the storm and collided with tragic results. He sadly concluded he would never see Captain Sam Patten or his fellow townsmen again.

For James Forsey and *Mary F. Harris* the fishing season ended quickly and unhappily, since the ship sustained storm damage and had to return to home port. There concerned relatives and the owners, Foote Brothers, anxiously awaited the arrival or news of *George Foote*. Captain Forsey had the heartbreaking task of relating the fate of the schooner and all her crew. He had been the last person to see *George Foote* through the spume and high seas as she prepared, like the *Cashier*, to beat the August Gale of 1892.

On September 26 a St. John's newspaper reported, albeit with no crew list, the disaster on the Grand Banks: "Besides the losses [already reported] from the effects of the storm, grave fears are entertained that *George Foote* of Grand Bank, Samuel Patten master, has been lost with all hands, comprising a crew of seventeen men. Captain George Brett arrived here [St. John's] a few days since, and reports having spoken to Captain James Forsey of *Mary F. Harris*, who said he was fishing in the same neighbourhood with *George Foote* and a Nova Scotian schooner and, when the storm was over, he saw the Nova Scotian at anchor, full of water with spars and sails gone. Near the same place he picked up a lot of wreckage, which evidently belonged to *George Foote*, and he came to the conclusion the two schooners collided, and the crews of both were drowned by the angry waves. But, as there is 'hope from the sea,' their friends cling to the idea they may have escaped in their dories, or the schooner became dismasted and is still driving about the ocean, and they will be rescued by some passing vessel."

While digging through archival papers some time after my initial conversation with Clyde Forsey, I located a reference to the loss of the LaHave schooner *Cashier*. News of *Cashier*'s wreck reached Nova Scotia in early September. By September 12, 1892, an article in *The Halifax Herald* reported she had been lost with her crew. The 107-ton *Cashier*, one of the finest vessels of the Nova Scotia fishing fleet, carried nineteen men. She was owned in LaHave by T.A. Wilson and Reinhardt Brothers and had been built in 1888 at Conquerall. Captain Alfred Reinhardt had previously captained the schooner *Cletia*, which his brother Benjamin now commanded. Three of the captain's brothers worked in LaHave; one was the collector of customs and two were in business.

Several of *Cashier*'s crew, many of whom lived in the LaHave area, were identified as: Captain Albert Reinhardt, aged 32; his brother-in-law whose last name was Pernette; two Legay brothers, Enus and Titus; George Richard, who left a family; Andrew (or Lewis Leander) Mosher, aged 19, of West Dublin; Eli Corkum, son of Sam Corkum, West Dublin; Spencer Remby, West Dublin; Howard Conrad; Benjamin Wagner; four men from Vogler's Cove whose names were not given; and a Wentzell of LaHave, about 50 years old who left a family of nine. Needless to say the people of LaHave, West Dublin, and neighbouring towns were devastated at the loss of *Cashier* and her entire crew. Once again a Nova Scotian town that sent a fleet of ships down to the sea had paid a heavy price for the riches of the ocean.

The September 12, 1892, issue of *The Halifax Herald* reported the loss of *Cashier*. No report has been located which identifies *George Foote*'s crew with the exception of two men: her captain Samuel Patten and Leonard Hartling, whose gravestones stand in Grand Bank, Newfoundland.

Shelburne crew wrecked at Fourchu, stranded at Sydney

At most major world seaports — New York, Boston, London and Liverpool, England, St. John's, and Halifax — there was a building, usually called the Seamen's Institute or Home, which was an important place for sailors especially those shipwrecked or awaiting transportation home. Not only was the institute a place to relax, play cards, get mail, and meet other sailors, but for mariners stranded it provided a haven where one could wash, shave and clean up. Many had a dormitory where clean beds were available at little or no cost. It was the lack of such a facility at Sydney, Nova Scotia, that gave the shipwrecked crew of *Sandolphin* cause to complain in August 1892.

The fishing schooner *Sandolphin*, commanded by Captain Bradford Thorburn and crewed by sixteen men from Shelburne, had about 200 quintals (approximately 22,400 pounds) of fish in the hold by August 11. On August 4, one of her dories with two men had disappeared; apparently they had drifted away while fishing and hopefully would reach safety. After a fruitless search for the two men, *Sandolphin* sailed for the nearest port and was off Fourchu Bay in relatively good weather when disaster struck. She went ashore at Bear Cove Point, Cape Breton.

The story of what happened next is best told by one of her crew, William Thompson: "On the day we went ashore — August 11, 1892 — there was a heavy fog and calm water with a long swell and strong currents. We were attempting to make harbour, but the current carried us to the leeward and with the log giving us twenty-six miles yet to run, we were on the breakers. We had to leave the schooner at once without securing much more than what we had on, as within a half hour after striking she was bilged and was a total loss. We stayed in the dories all night and next morning went ashore, some of us going one way and some another. A house was found where the residents told us of the town of Fourchu being only a mile and a half to the eastward. We went there in our dories and were kindly received and hospitably treated till Wednesday, August 17, on which morning we all set out for South Sydney, a distance of forty miles."

William Thompson went on to describe how they travelled to South Sydney — a few by horse teams and the majority on foot. Thompson and *Sandolphin*'s cook travelled by a light wagon so that they would arrive in South Sydney first. He had a letter with him, written by the Customs Collector at Fourchu addressed to the Collector at South Sydney, Ronald MacDonald. The letter was intended to have accommodations and arrangements prepared for the remaining fourteen of *Sandolphin*'s crew when they reached South Sydney. Thompson arrived about five p.m., went straight to MacDonald's residence and handed him the letter.

What happened next, as told by Thompson, astonished him and subsequently the rest of the crew: "[MacDonald] read it and said he could do nothing for us. He said he would go to the telegraph office and wire the Marine and Fisheries [Department]. Whether he did I know not, but he said there was nothing to be done and we would have to shift for ourselves.

"He, however, prevailed on two old women, their domicile a hovel, to agree to receive our crowd who arrived about nine o'clock in the evening. Some of our shipwrecked crew, a lad in particular, were so bad they had to be supported by the others, due to the exertion of walking nineteen miles on a country road without boots. We got nothing to eat that night and slept on the floor. In the morning there was no breakfast and we were getting desperate. A policeman, a blacksmith, and a minister, I think Rev. Dr. Smith, gave us food, about now for the want of which much longer some of us would have died. A lawyer had the case called to his attention and he succeeded in showing to collector MacDonald the right of human beings to be kindly treated."

The young boy of *Sandolphin*, although weak from his ordeal of shipwreck, rescue, travel on foot with no shoes, starvation and fatigue, recovered. But Captain Thorburn, Thompson and the rest of *Sandolphin*'s crew agreed it was the worst treatment they had ever experienced.

But their disgust and disappointment turned to joy when on their journey to Halifax they met their two missing shipmates from *Sandolphin*, mate Elijah McLeod and Frederick Armstrong. McLeod and Armstrong had left the ship to haul their trawl and met with the often-told privations — adrift in an open dory without food or water. They were picked up by the Lunenburg schooner *Sadie* and transferred to the ship *Atlanta* bound for Canso. They travelled on the same train to Halifax as their shipwrecked companions but, up to the time of the meeting, McLeod and Armstrong had not known *Sandolphin* was wrecked. By August 23, they all had arrived in Halifax and were lodged in the Sailors' Home, a place of refuge for shipwrecked sailors.

But, as the saying goes, it's an ill wind that doesn't blow some good. The plight of *Sandolphin*'s men launched a public outcry. An appeal sent to the Nova Scotian government was also published in the local paper. In essence it stated, "Send shipwrecked crews to their homes without delay."

Stranded sailors, whether on foreign shores or in their own country, were often destitute and dependent on welfare and handouts. Usually they had no ship and no income. Finding accommodations and arranging for transportation home were serious problems not only for unmarried seamen but especially for those with families to support.

The reporter for *The Halifax Herald* recalled the newspaper raising money to help send stranded Canadian or Newfoundland fishermen home — the case of *Sandolphin*'s crew being only the most recent. Shipwrecked crews of American vessels were looked after by the United States consulate, but there was no provision for Canadian seamen.

Two wrecks at Westport and Parrsboro

Less than two months later, on October 8, the schooner *Alfred* commanded by Captain Outhouse left Westport headed for the fishing grounds. While off Dartmouth Point, Digby County, the wind slackened, she struck rocks and went to pieces. The crew of twelve escaped, but *Alfred* valued at $1,300 remained on the shoreline as debris. She was owned by E.C. Bowers, John Snow of Digby, and Captain Outhouse of Westport.

The story of the end of *Rossignol* is a two-fold wreck. *Rossignol* was a vessel of 1,509 tons, registered and built at Tusket in 1872. Although Yarmouth was her home port, she was owned by T.G. Soley and Company of Liverpool, England. On October 1, while under command of Captain Fulton, *Rossignol* was bound from Parrsboro to England laden with lumber when she stranded on Spencer's Island in the Bay of Fundy. The next day she was towed to West Bay to be surveyed. Then, on the sixth, the tug *Neptune* towed *Rossignol* to Partridge Island in the Minas Basin. On October 7, while Captain Fulton was away from his ship making arrangements for repairs, the wind came up. By the time he reached the wharf, his ship was nowhere to be found. Apparently *Rossignol* had parted her moorings in the wind and tide, drifted around Cape Split and went ashore in Scots Bay. She drove upon the rocks to total loss.

The Yarmouth waterfront in 1872 shows the Killam Brothers' barque *Lima* (far left) and the Young, Kinney and Corning ship *Rossignol* outfitting on the docks. (Unidentified newspaper clipping)

No survivors on Mabou schooner

There were no survivors to tell the tale. But the loss of a schooner at the mouth of Halifax harbour on November 6, 1894, can be told through the words of an eye witness to the tragic event, William Johnson of Bear Cove: "Shortly before six a.m. I saw a vessel off Herring Cove. She was double reefed and the captain was evidently trying to bring her about to keep her off the land. I saw the difficulty she was in and watched her. The vessel was drifting toward Bear Cove (near Halifax harbour) and they were doing their utmost to bring her about, but to no avail. There was a strong breeze and heavy rain, but this was not the worst feature; it was the heavy seas which dashed her against the rocks."

Slowly the vessel drifted toward the rocks and those on board must have had death staring them in the face. If they were to strike in such a sea only a miracle could save them.

It was the 48-ton schooner *Annie M. Pride* which had left Mabou on October 19 with a cargo of 800 quintals (89,600 pounds) of fish consigned to Boak & Bennett. When the cargo had been landed at Halifax *Annie M. Pride* left for Mabou, on the western side of Cape Breton. Up to early November the fall weather had been excellent, but it rapidly deteriorated by midnight on November 5. Just before midnight the signal men at the Halifax Citadel reported a furious gale approaching from the east. Within an hour the barometer dropped to 28.40 and wind increased to hurricane force.

Early on the morning of November 6 reports came in of a ship — which proved to be *Annie M. Pride* — lost with all crew at the mouth of the harbour. Johnson described her final minutes: "The vessel got to within thirty feet of the shore when she was fairly lifted from the water and dashed against the rocks with such force that she was broken in two, and she immediately went over and sank. From the time the vessel struck and went down was less than a couple of minutes. It happened so quickly that it was not possible to render any assistance. Even had rescuers been able to reach the ship, there would not have been time to help.

"I saw nobody on board from the time the vessel was first sighted. I then went along the shore, directly opposite to where she struck; she was only a few feet away. I could see her bowsprit, anchor, and her stern, but the remainder of the vessel was all in pieces. I tried to see if there was any sign of any person on board, but did not. When the vessel struck the men were likely all below, and I do not think they were drowned, but were killed when the vessel dashed against the rocks. There were a number of empty casks come ashore, and also a few fish."

When *Annie M. Pride* left Halifax for Mabou, those who sailed on her were Captain James J. Pride, aged 38 of St. Mary's; Bernard Pride, 11, the captain's son; Charles Young of England who had once resided in Halifax; and Joseph Morris, a Newfoundlander. Captain Pride, well known in Halifax, had taken his son Bernard with him for a pleasure trip while his other two children resided with Mrs. Ring of Cornwallis Street. The vessel was insured for $1,500 with Nova Scotia Marine. By November 9, four bodies had been recovered from the wreck — Captain Pride and seaman Morris while the other two were not named. In the inquest into the tragedy, Coroner Finn of Halifax verified all four had drowned.

Every sea disaster has its own footnotes and the wreck of *Annie M. Pride* is no exception: the cook of the schooner failed to make the trip. He had owed three small bills in Halifax, credit extended for food for the vessel. Apparently the captain paid two bills, but refused to pay the third and thus the cook, to show his displeasure, quit and did not sail.

In addition to the wreck of the Mabou schooner, several other ships encountered the full force of the gale, including the troopship *Tyne* and the steamers *Sylvia*, *St. Pierre* and *Pro Patria*. Two barques, *Ida B* and *Clara*, were known to have left Halifax a few hours before the storm. All six reported safely.

Tragedy at Digby Gut, Victoria Beach

As the news trickled in of shipping losses on Nova Scotia's eastern coast, there came reports of fatalities at Digby Gut in the Bay of Fundy. The Yarmouth schooner *Annie May*, caught in the gale of November 6-7, had been sailing from Parrsboro to Boston laden with lumber. For a day the 86-ton schooner and her five crewmen, under the capable leadership of Captain Hatfield, withstood the worst of nature's elements. Somewhere off Digby, as Hatfield struggled to keep the vessel's head to the sea, the tremendous winds tore the sails away rendering *Annie May* unmanageable.

On the evening of November 6, the captain decided to beach the schooner before nightfall. As the crew prepared, the main mast shattered killing one man. As *Annie May* grounded against the rocks, about three miles east of Digby Gut, her deck load of lumber went overboard in a tangled mess taking two other men to their deaths. Captain Hatfield stood by his vessel as long as possible, holding the wheel though seas were constantly breaking over him. Seeing the last of his men washed overboard, he lashed himself to the main gaff and reached shore barely conscious with severe lacerations and bruises.

When Hatfield recovered somewhat he staggered for the nearest house, three miles distant. Without a coat or hat and in bare feet over rocks and snow drifts, he stumbled and crawled until he saw a light — the home of Joseph White, Victoria Beach. White immediately cared for the delirious man and then set out to get help for *Annie May*'s crew, if any were still alive. But it was too late; Hatfield was the only survivor. Lost were a Harris from Canning, a man from Parrsboro, and another from Yarmouth.

Before the storm blew itself out on November 8, the Gloucester, Massachusetts, schooner *Monitor* beached at Whitehead but was later refloated. *Gaza*, a schooner commanded by Captain McClellan of Minudie and bound for Port Greville, went ashore at Margaretville in the Bay of Fundy. *Gaza* lost her cargo of hay and her foremast. Her steering gear was destroyed making the 40-ton schooner, which was uninsured, an easy victim of wind and waves. Her crew — Captain McClellan, Alex Collins and Abraham McCully — barely escaped with their lives.

D. Landry of Petit-de-Grat reported his schooner, *Kezia*, ashore at Petit-de-Grat with five feet of water in her holds. Landry and his crew were bound from New York to Charlottetown. *Kezia*, at 130 tons and built at Conquerall in 1882, was a total wreck. Fortunately she was insured through China Mutual for $3,000.

Wrecks on Yarmouth coast

In the days of sail, Yarmouth, a historic port founded more than 200 years ago, always sent a vast fleet of vessels to sea. At one period in its history it was the largest shipping port, per capita, in Canada. Hundreds of sailing ships and scores of steamers were owned there and the numerous Yarmouth ships lost at sea took many lives with them. The rugged coast near Yarmouth claimed the town's own ships as well as foreign vessels. Several were large, well-known ships and the tragic circumstances surrounding the disasters became news headlines across Canada.

One of the most dramatic events occurred on March 11, 1899, when the British-built Allan Line steamer *Castilian*, captained by Joseph Barrett, piled onto the southwest point of Gannet Rock Ledges, thirteen miles from the Yarmouth lighthouse. Only recently launched, *Castilian* was the largest steamer to have been wrecked on a Canadian coastline up to that time. She was 470 feet long and carried a crew of 104. *Castilian*'s hold held a rich bounty for salvagers and much was landed at Yarmouth: nearly 100,000 bushels of wheat, more than 68,000 bushels of corn, thousands of cases of canned goods, and eighteen thoroughbred horses. The old Cann Steamship Line put three tugs on the site of the wreck to transfer goods to port, taking several days to finish the work.

The passenger and freight paddle steamer *City of Monticello* foundered on November 10, 1900, five miles from Yarmouth, (Photo courtesy Captain Hubert Hall, Shipsearch Marine, Yarmouth)

Another wreck near Yarmouth made world news. On November 10, 1900, *City of Monticello* foundered in the Bay of Fundy. An iron paddle steamer of 470 tons owned by Yarmouth Steamship Company, *City of Monticello* operated a passenger and mail service between Yarmouth and Saint John. When she went down only four of the forty people aboard survived; the captain, Thomas Harding, went down with his ship. One of the mail bags later drifted in at Pinkney's Point, Yarmouth County.

The amount of salvage and loss of life on the *City of Monticello* reminded people around Yarmouth of the loss of *Hungarian* many years before. On February 19, 1860, *Hungarian* went ashore near Cape Sable Island on Black Head Ledge with the loss of her entire crew and passengers — many accounts put the number at more than 300 lives.

Hungarian, a steam packet first owned by Montreal Ocean Steamship Company that later became the Allan Line of transatlantic steamers, was registered at 1,487 tons. With his crew of eighty, Captain Oliver Jones commanded this great ship which carried more than 120 passengers, including forty-six accommodated in her elaborate cabins. She struck on the ledges about two miles from Cape Sable. The few people watching from the shore had only small open boats that could not withstand the heavy breakers and surf. Scores clung to *Hungarian*'s rigging and one by one exposure claimed them. As the ship disintegrated and the masts eventually broke, other victims fell into the sea. There were no survivors and no bodies drifted ashore. One eye witness claimed, "The waters around the wreck were alive with dogfish."

A group of investors in Yarmouth purchased *Hungarian's* hull and valuable cargo of dry goods for £4,000. From her holds came many bolts of fine silk and cloth. Local Yarmouth ships cashed in and it was claimed that there was hardly a woman in southwestern Nova Scotia who did not have a silk dress made from this cloth.

The Great Lakes freighter *Thordoc*, built in 1908 and netting 1,375 tons, was wrecked at Winging Point, near Louisbourg on March 30, 1940. (Photo courtesy C.F. McBride and Shipsearch Marine, Captain Hubert Hall, Yarmouth)

Chapter 3 (1903–12)
Early catastrophes

Wreck of *Gold Seeker* of Liverpool

On July 12, 1903, A. W. Hendry and Son of Liverpool received the news from Colon, Columbia, of the loss of their schooner *Gold Seeker* and three of her Nova Scotian crew.

Gold Seeker, built in Liverpool in 1896, was a topsail schooner of 199 tons commanded by Captain George Diggdon of Port Medway. She was last reported seen on June 4, sailing from Barbados for Grenada with the intention of obtaining a cargo of coconuts to be delivered to New York.

In a heavy squall during the night of July 2, the schooner capsized and sank while ten miles east-northeast of the Isle of Pinos in the Caribbean Sea. Three of *Gold Seeker*'s crew were drowned: mate Arthur Frellick, about 45 and a resident of Western Head where he left a wife and eight children; bosun James Moore was a native of Brooklyn who resided in Mill Village with his wife; and the cook, William Downey, who had a wife and young family, was born in Liverpool but lived in Lockeport. The captain and the remainder of the crew travelled back to Nova Scotia via a ship bound for New York.

Derelict at Duncan's Ledges

The 137-ton schooner *Onora* was making her way from Puerto Rico to Nova Scotia with a cargo of molasses. Built in Bridgetown, Nova Scotia, in 1890, the 96-foot long *Onora* was once owned by C.B. Whidden of Antigonish who had sold her to Longley and Company of Halifax. Upon delivery of her cargo to G.P. Mitchell and Sons, Longley planned to sell the schooner in St. Pierre. She carried a mixed crew: Captain John Atkinson and seaman Long hailed from New Brunswick; Archibald Baird, aged 21, of St. John's, Newfoundland; two sailors were European, while the lone Nova Scotian aboard was cook John F. Bowden of Guysborough.

She left Puerto Rico April 9, 1904. In late April one of the Halifax pilot boats sighted *Onora* five miles off Sambro but as the schooner did not signal for a pilot, the boat did not approach her. The wind was light but a heavy sea pounded the shore.

On Friday, April 29, a derelict ship with no sign of life was discovered in Duncan's Cove. Closer investigation identified the wreck as *Onora* and her battered lifeboat had been located on shore. The previous night had been exceptionally dark, thus it was presumed the sea had pushed the schooner close to the hidden, treacherous Duncan's Ledges that extend from shore for quite a distance. She was about six miles from where the pilot boat had spotted her.

Only one body was recovered. On Saturday, Daniel Connors of Duncan's Cove located Baird's remains, fully dressed, boots on but not laced and the bottom of his trousers tucked inside of his socks. No other bodies were discovered and it was presumed all aboard *Onora* had perished.

Authorities believed that if the crew had stayed aboard the vessel and not taken to the lifeboat they would have been rescued by the crew of a passing tugboat. When the tug *Whitney* arrived in port Saturday morning, *Onora* was still holding on the ledge with her deck out of water, masts standing and the foresail and three jibs were up. That evening in stronger wind and greater wave action, she had moved from her position. The derelict was pounding on the rocks and the sea breaking over her sent foam half the height of her masts. According to the tug's Captain Landry, it was impossible to board *Onora* and her cargo, including 256 puncheons of molasses, was spilling out and drifting to shore.

Edward Johnson, a justice of the peace, convened an inquiry/autopsy jury on Saturday evening to examine Baird's body which returned a verdict of "found drowned." Undertaker Spencer prepared Baird's body for burial.

In the strong winds of Sunday evening, the masts pounded out and *Onora* was reduced to debris along the shore.

Lockeport captain lost

A.W. Hendry and Son of Liverpool received a brief message on November 12, 1909, that another of their foreign fleet of schooners had met with disaster. Six years previously *Gold Seeker* had been wrecked with the loss of three of her crew, and now the information out of New York indicated *John S. Bennett* had gone to the bottom taking several crew members with her.

Somewhere off Block Island in the state of Rhode Island, *John S. Bennett*, a 300-ton barquentine, collided with the four-masted schooner *Merrill C. Hart*. *Hart* went down with all hands; of *Bennett*'s crew of eight, two survived. The only witnesses, Captain Bullock and the men on the *William Jones*, came upon the scene several minutes after the collision. Bullock reported that about one a.m. on November 8, he was passing Block Island and noticed a vessel's lights nearby. He approached close enough to speak to her. The captain hailed him and asked for assistance, calling out that his vessel had been in a collision and was sinking.

Bullock immediately came about and readied a lifeboat to go to the rescue of the barquentine. Before the boat could be put over the side, the barquentine had sunk; some bits of wreckage were all that could be seen floating in the vicinity. Close by searchers located two Filipinos clinging to a small boat and picked them up. At first nothing could be learned about what had happened for the survivors spoke no English. Bullock scoured the area but found no trace of other survivors. By now it was daylight and although Bullock looked for other vessels in the vicinity he saw nothing. *William Jones*, bound for New York with a cargo of lumber, sped with full sail to her destination, not only to report the disaster but to find someone to question the two survivors in their own language.

At New York, through an interpreter, the Filipinos told their story. They related how their vessel, *John S. Bennett*, had collided with a four-master and within a few minutes the four-master sank. Soon the details of *Bennett*'s identity became clear. Owned in Liverpool, she was crewed mostly by Nova Scotians, none of whom survived: Captain Jonas Firth, first mate Hadley, second mate Aubrey Geldert, all of Lockeport, cook Daniel Stoutley, and two other seamen whose names were not recorded.

Given the details in the survivors' story and by examining the floating remains of the two ships, investigators tried to piece together what had happened. Apparently the barquentine *Bennett*, the larger vessel, ran upon the schooner in the night. The *Merrill C. Hart*, which had been in regular service around Maine for forty-three years, was smashed to pieces and went down immediately. Although old, she had recently been rebuilt and was laden with a cargo of stone. *Merrill C. Hart* carried a crew of five, including Captain Charles C. Boles of Tennant's Harbor, Maine.

By November 9 and 10, some debris drifted ashore between Block Island and the Rhode Island mainland: a smashed boat, the top of a deck-house, a quarter board bearing the name "Merrill C. Hart," a fog horn of foreign make operated by a crank, a number of doors, and a considerable number of whole and splintered planks — all thought to have come from the schooner. Also found was a photograph, apparently of a Filipino — that alone came from the *John S. Bennett*.

Ruby, the hazards of fishing

Ruby, captained by Josiah Hiscock of Grand Bank, Newfoundland, and crewed by Placentia Bay fishermen, had been fishing on Quero Bank but ran out of bait. While attempting to enter Louisbourg harbour on May 23, 1910, the 71-ton banking schooner ran ashore on Fourchu Point, near Louisbourg. Her cargo of 900 quintals (about 100,800 pounds) of fish was not insured, but the vessel itself, worth $4,000 and owned by Samuel Harris of Grand Bank, was covered by the Grand Bank Mutual Insurance Company.

Paddy Dober of Little Bay, Newfoundland, was one of the crew and his younger brother James was his dorymate. After *Ruby* struck the rocks and the dories were launched, Jim was not quite ready to step aboard. In the rush to abandon ship, someone grabbed Jim and threw him aboard the dory, injuring his knee — an injury he bore for the rest of his life. Hiscock, the Dobers and the remaining crew reached Louisbourg safely, but Harris' schooner broke up on Nova Scotian shores. Hiscock survived this wreck, but in February 1917 he disappeared with his crew and the schooner *John McRea* off Newfoundland's southern Avalon Peninsula.

Cora, victim of Petrie's Ledge

On November 10, 1910, while Captain George Hickman attempted to make port at North Sydney at night, the schooner *Cora* struck and grounded on Petrie's Ledge outside the harbour. At the time, it seemed fortunate that she stranded at low tide, making it likely that with high water the next morning the schooner would be refloated. It was not to be. By the time the harbour tug *Iona* steamed down to pull the stranded *Cora* off the shoal, the heavy sea and strong wind had strained her timbers. By the next day, *Cora* disintegrated rapidly at the entrance to North Sydney.

Julia Forsey, a wreck at Cranberry Head

Bound from North Sydney to Lamaline, Newfoundland, with a cargo of coal, the schooner *Julia Forsey* ran ashore at Cranberry Head, Nova Scotia, on May 31, 1908. During the previous few months, the scene had been the site of several wrecks. Veteran shipping men around the coast were of the opinion that the removal of the fog whistle on Cranberry Head had been the cause, and advocated it should be brought back and that a beacon should also be installed.

Sudden storms had forced Captain Charles Hillier of Fortune, Newfoundland, to attempt to take the 63-ton schooner back to port for shelter when she stranded. Built in 1880 at Grand Bank and owned by G. & A. Buffett, *Julia Forsey*, at the time of her loss, was valued at $1,250.

In early August 1908 a German cruiser S.M.S. *Freya* struck the Gloucester fishing vessel *Maggie and May* sixty miles southeast of Halifax. The schooner, which carried several Nova Scotian and Newfoundland seamen, sank in two minutes. The disaster happened at 11:30 p.m. and darkness probably contributed to the great loss of life. The German crew rescued Silvian White, John Muse (or Muise), William Muse all of Eel Brook, Yarmouth County, and Leo Farn of Belleoram, Newfoundland. Appendix C lists those who died in the collision.

S.S. " Bruce," the Connecting Link between Canada and Newfoundland

Both a passenger and freight ferry between Port aux Basques and North Sydney for fourteen years (2,000 round trips), S.S. *Bruce* (above) came to an end near Port Nova, eight miles from Louisbourg. North Sydney harbour was blocked with ice. On the snowy night of March 24, 1911, *Bruce* encountered drift ice and was pushed off course. A lookout mistook the light on Scaterie for a similar light at Louisbourg. At 4:45 a.m. she struck rocks. Captain Drake ordered the lifeboats over and in the process two Newfoundlanders drowned: William Pike of St. Lawrence and a man named Shea of Brigus or Carbonear. The other 128 passengers and twenty-seven crew members reached shore safely. The Dominion Coal Company steamer *Louisbourg* and the tug *Douglas H. Thomas* reached the scene first and brought the survivors to Louisbourg. On the evening of the wreck the *Bruce* broke apart in the centre. No mail bags or freight were saved. (Photo taken from a postcard)

Halvdan's crew reach Sydney

On October 22, 1911, the steamer *Halvdan* of Norway stranded on Bad Neighbour Shoal near St. Esprit while navigating in dense fog off Framboise. Immediately her forward holds filled with water. *Halvdan*, on her maiden voyage, was en route from Chile to Montreal heavily laden with nitroglycerine. She netted 2,400 tons but with her heavy load was 7,000 tons dead weight. When the news of the wreck reached Sydney, the tug *Douglas H. Thomas* left to assist the twenty-six crewmen.

Halvdan hit about three a.m. in thick fog, but fortunately for the crew the sea was smooth and there was little wind. She grounded on a well-known and particularly dangerous shoal, located about two miles offshore. Surrounding the ledges are ten fathoms of water, whereas the rocks themselves are covered with two fathoms. Strong currents sweep the coast which probably pushed *Halvdan* off course.

As soon as *Halvdan* struck, the foc'sle head filled with water and Captain Gerdesen ordered the lifeboats launched. The crew remained around the ship all night, then at daylight rowed to land. Every two or three hours during Sunday and Sunday night they rowed out to the stricken *Halvdan* until officially abandoning her at eight a.m. Monday.

The motorboat *Luxor* brought the crew to Louisbourg, then they travelled by train to Sydney where they stayed in the Savoy Hotel. After an inquiry held on October 28, presided over by J.E. Burchell, no blame was placed on the young captain who had been working and commanding ships on the coal run between Sydney and Montreal for several years. The crew, all placed on Norwegian vessels that frequented Nova Scotia, eventually went home or found employment on other ships.

Wrecks at Yarmouth and Isaac's Harbour

The tern schooner *Reliance*, under Captain Loemer, left Philadelphia in early November, 1911, with a cargo of 400 tons of coal for L.E. Baker and Company. On November 13 she sailed into Yarmouth harbour to avoid a gale and heavy sea. *Reliance*, built in 1906 in Shelburne by George A. Cox, drifted onto a ledge north of the Hen and Chickens buoy at the entrance to Yarmouth. The crew was taken off and landed safely on shore by the Sandy Point lifesaving crew. The gale force wind and waves soon reduced the tern to matchwood.

Less than a month later at Isaac's Harbour, the schooner *Loyal* from Summerside, Prince Edward Island, and laden with produce for Liverpool was wrecked. She tried to make Isaac's Harbour in the snowstorm raging over Cape Breton on December 3, but ran aground on the back of Harbour Island. Exposed to the elements, *Loyal* filled with water. S.R. Griffin and Son sent some men in a small boat to the stricken schooner, to salvage what they could from the deck load of bagged oats and cedar shingles before the ship broke up. *Loyal*, not insured, was registered to her captain, Hutchison, and his father of Richibucto, New Brunswick. The cargo was owned by J.W. Smith of Liverpool and by George Smith who sailed on the schooner.

Maitland and Economy vessels lost same night

Their sails blown away and their dories swept over the side by raging seas, two coasting schooners were driven ashore in a November gale in 1911. The crews barely escaped a watery grave. One, *Wanita* hailing from Economy, grounded near Spencer's Island on Wednesday night, November 15; then before the next morning, the Maitland schooner *Shamrock* went ashore in the Bay of Fundy.

Headed for New Brunswick with potatoes, *Wanita* stripped of sail made a brave stand against the elements. Without power she wallowed helplessly in the frenzied ocean while her captain tried to get her into the lee of Spencer's Island in the Minas Basin, Bay of Fundy. A shift in wind bore her onto a beach near Spencer's Island. After *Wanita* struck, the seas broke over her and the captain and crew clung to the wreck expecting each minute to be washed off the hulk. With the assistance of people on the shore, they made it safely to land.

The second vessel, *Shamrock*, was wrecked when the wind veered to westward the next day. When close to the shore the captain ordered both anchors dropped but, with the strong wind and heavy seas, they failed to hold. *Shamrock* drifted onto a rock, stern first, which tore away her rudder. By then she was a hundred yards or so from shore and continued to bump and grind. Feeling she would break apart the captain ordered both cables slipped; but *Shamrock* drifted in to shore, a total wreck. The crew made land safely.

Two steamers collide off Country Harbour

In late December 1911 a sea tragedy unfolded ten miles off Country Harbour, Guysborough County, when two steamers collided.

S.S. *Renwick*, bound from Port Hastings for Halifax with a cargo of a thousand tons of coal, made good time in the early morning of December 28. *Renwick* had left Port Hastings at seven p.m. and had clear sailing and a smooth voyage up to the time of the collision. At 2:45 in the morning, while ten miles off Country Harbour, the men on watch saw the lights of another steamer which they eventually learned was the S.S. *St. Pierre-Miquelon*.

St. Pierre-Miquelon, a French mail steamer out of St. Pierre, had a full head of steam en route from Halifax to North Sydney and due to return to St. Pierre. According to one of the twelve men who escaped the ensuing wreck, *St. Pierre-Miquelon* veered her course slightly but with enough change in direction that she ploughed into the side of the smaller *Renwick*.

Built in England in 1892, *Renwick*, about 400 tons, was owned by the Inverness Railway and Coal Company (McKenzie and Mann) and had been used in the Port Hastings coal trade for several years. Although her cargo was insured, no insurance was carried on the ship. The Nova Scotian steamer took the impact a little forward of amidships — a blow which almost cut her in two. Captain J.F. Chapman and those on *Renwick*'s deck immediately launched one of the ship's boats, sounded alarms and abandoned ship. In five minutes *Renwick* went down, taking three of her crew with her. Three firemen who were below deck — Edward McGolderick of Parrsboro, Morgan Hann aged 24 from Port aux Basques but a resident of Halifax, and Karl Fenz of Germany — had no chance for their lives and perished. William Wiggerton, a native of England residing in Port Hastings, was first listed as a victim but this was an error. The confusion arose from the knowledge that his brother had served on *Renwick* up to her last trip.

According to the survivors' story, they could see no effort made by the captain and crew of *St. Pierre-Miquelon* to rescue the men on the fast-sinking *Renwick*. The sole means of survival came from their own quick actions when they launched the ship's lifeboat. Chapman would make no statement on the cause nor would he blame anyone until the matter came before the courts.

After *Renwick* had gone to the bottom Captain Chapman and his crew were taken aboard the French steamer which continued its journey to North Sydney. The survivors — Captain Chapman of Dartmouth (the son-in-law of Captain George May of the ferry *Dartmouth*), first officer William A. Poole, second officer Angus Rudolf, chief engineer Edward Meehan (brother of James Meehan of the Stairs, Son and Morrow firm), second engineer George A. Miller, steward Robert Forrester, cook Percy Barnett, seamen L. Bragg, Allan Chapman, Larry Fahey, Abraham Hansen, and another unidentified fireman — arrived in North Sydney about six p.m. Those crewmen who belonged to Port Hastings left that night for home.

While the above photo is probably not the steamer *Renwick*, it serves to illustrate the type and size of these ships. The freighter shown served the North Shore of Cape Breton Island and is docked at Sainthill's Wharf, North Sydney. The schooner *Palfrey*, tied on by the steamer, is laden with barrels of oil and supplies destined for Newfoundland. (Photo courtesy North Sydney Museum)

John Harvey — two lives lost at Gabarus

The Belleoram-built tern *John Harvey* was wrecked on Nova Scotian shores. On January 10, 1912, while bound from Gloucester, Massachusetts, to St. Pierre with general cargo, she struck Winning Point four miles from Gabarus during a gale described as hurricane force.

She grounded a tantalizingly short distance from shore: so close yet too far to swim in the cold water. With her dories smashed or useless, one of her eight crewmen, John Keeping of Belleoram, Newfoundland, knew it was better to die in an attempt of self-rescue than to give up and to go down with the ship. He swam to the shore with a line around his waist so that Captain George Kearley and the rest of the crew — two of whom were Kearley's sons — could reach land safely. When the others reached the shore, they found Keeping had died of exposure and hypothermia. Another seaman, John Foote also of Belleoram, perished on the shores of Gabarus that day. The remaining six men found shelter in fishing shacks until people of Gabarus located them. They later walked to Louisbourg where the story of the heroic sailors was made public.

Stanzas three to seven of the folk song "The Loss of the *John Harvey*," taken from John P. Parker's book *Sails of the Maritimes*, describes the event:

> The skipper gave orders to his men,
> The vessel to dismast her,
> The boats were frozen to the deck
> As the seas swept fore-and-after.
> Said Captain Kearley to his men,
> "My boys, it is no use,
> I fear that we are doomed to die
> On the shores of Gabarus."
>
> Then young John Keeping, a rope he took,
> And tied it round his waist,
> Said he would swim for the nearest land,
> And the icy foam he faced.
> Oh, bitterly cold was that winter's night,
> The seas rolled mountains high,
> All tossed and battered by the wave
> Was that bold Belleoram boy.

The wind it blew a hurricane,
The night was bitter cold,
'Twould chill the heart of a sailor lad,
A hero young and bold.
When tossed and battered by the sea,
He at last the shore did reach,
And with his badly frozen hands
Made fast a line to the beach.

The crew of the *Harvey* got ashore,
There were six of them all told,
They owe their lives to God above,
And the Keeping boy so bold.
But Keeping and the brave young Foote
By exhaustion overcome,
Died on the shores of Gabarus
Far from their native home.

The survivors walked to some fishing shacks,
That stood along the shore,
Much hampered by their heavy boots,
And the oilskins that they wore.
They had no match to light a fire,
How awful was their plight,
As they struggled for existence
On that cold winter's night.

The same storm that wrecked *John Harvey* played havoc on other Nova Scotian shores. The schooner *Virginia* was a total loss at Rose Head, a rocky cape between Lunenburg and the mouth of the LaHave River. Captain Leander Publicover and his crew of six sailed with the ship in ballast from Halifax to Liverpool to load lumber for Barbados. Battered by the gale that swept the coast, *Virginia*, owned by A.C. Barnaby of Bridgewater, was pushed onto the rocks and wrecked. She had been built in Lunenburg seven years previously and was insured at LaHave Marine Insurance for $3,000.

An American torpedo boat, *Terry*, was off Cape Sable when the storm struck. With her holds flooded, *Terry* was disabled and at the mercy of the seas for two days with white water pouring over her decks. All bedding and clothing was soaked and no food could be cooked so the eighty-two sailors lived on canned food.

The gale, which lasted for several days, had winds estimated to be in excess of fifty miles per hour from the southeast veering to the southwest. The Dartmouth ferry *Halifax* was nearly wrecked off the Dockyard in Halifax harbour. When Captain Arnold asked to have all passengers taken off, the tug *Scotsman* made fast to *Halifax* with cables and the passengers transferred to the tug. They were landed safely at Central Wharf.

Wrecked at St. Mary's Bay, Grand Passage

Exactly one month after the loss of *John Harvey*, a Yarmouth-owned vessel wrecked while trying to round Southern Point making for Westport. This was the 148-ton schooner *Mina German*, only two years old and built at Meteghan. At midnight and during a thick snowstorm, *Mina German* grounded at the St. Mary's Bay entrance to Grand Passage. Although the steamer *Westport* made three attempts to pull her off, the vessel remained firm.

Owner Captain Thomas German of Meteghan was in Annapolis when he heard of the wreck and he went immediately to Digby and thence for Westport. *Mina German* had been bound to Puerto Rico from Weymouth with a cargo of lumber. Both cargo and vessel were insured.

Crew of Liverpool schooner rescued

When the cable ship *Mackay-Bennett* arrived back in Halifax on February 11, 1912, her decks were covered in ice and she carried two crews: her own and six men from the tern schooner *Caledonia*.

A vessel of 188 tons, *Caledonia*, commanded by Captain Clarence Shrader, had left Lunenburg for New York on Tuesday of the previous week. She was deeply laden with lumber, but *Caledonia* was well equipped to handle the load had she not encountered a typical winter storm on Thursday. During the storm *Caledonia* sprang a leak; the crew manned the pumps, but water in her holds rose steadily. Realizing the gravity of the situation, the captain headed toward LaHave Landing, about 150 miles to the southwest.

Friday morning, the second day of trouble, the forward part of the ship dipped. Water in the holds and heavily iced rigging pulled her down. Although the crew jettisoned the cargo, by the afternoon *Caledonia*'s decks were awash and the six men had to find refuge in the ice-coated rigging. Below them the sea pounded the decks of *Caledonia*, smashing the water casks and the dory and ripping off the deck gear. There was no way the crew could get to the deck or to the cabin for extra clothing, shelter, or for flares to signal a passing ship.

By five p.m. Friday, between gusts of snow, *Mackay-Bennett* saw the beleaguered tern. She manoeuvered alongside, took off the men, and fastened a cable to *Caledonia*. For two days and sixty miles the cable ship made slow but steady progress toward Halifax with the tern in tow. Then the tern capsized and had to be abandoned.

Captain Shrader expressed his relief and gratitude: "Had [we] not been rescued on Friday, it is very probable we would not have survived in the zero temperatures and bitter winds of Friday night. Captain Gardner of the *Mackay-Bennett* treated us with great hospitality and brought us back to land, instead of proceeding on his trip to repair cable. We especially grateful because we were out of the course of steamers and probably would not have been seen by any other boat. We lost all our belongings and had to borrow some clothing from the *Mackay-Bennett* sailors."

During the two-day ordeal, *Caledonia*'s mate endured a frost-bitten foot, while the cook was washed overboard when the tern was waterlogged. Fortunately he grabbed the fly rail and was saved, suffering only bruised ribs in his brush with death.

The tug *Scotsman* left Halifax to look for the capsized tern. *Caledonia* was registered to A.W. Hendry and Son of Liverpool and both cargo and vessel were insured. In the same month, February 1912, the Hendry interests had another ship missing — *Annie W. Hendry*, sixty days out from Turks Island in the West Indies to Lunenburg with a cargo of salt.

Built in 1884, the steamship *Mackay-Bennett* (above) was used as a cable ship, mostly out of Halifax, until 1922. She was used as a cable storage hulk at Plymouth, England, and was scrapped in 1965. In this photo, taken in the early 1900s, she is tied up at Halifax alongside a pier filled with navigation buoys and cordwood. In April 1912 she sailed to the site of the *Titanic* sinking and helped recover 328 bodies, 209 of those were brought to Halifax. (Photo courtesy Captain Hubert Hall, Shipsearch Marine, Yarmouth)

seamen all wished to find more work on the ocean. Two shipped on with *Mackay-Bennett* while the others, destitute, looked for work. Two were Nova Scotians, two Newfoundlanders, one Swede, and the other from Chile.

About two months after this rescue, *Mackay-Bennett* was involved in another sea misadventure, which brought her more fame although she recovered no one alive. She was among the first to reach the site of the *Titanic* disaster south of Cape Race, Newfoundland. For three weeks she stayed there, pulling bodies from the ocean. Many were brought to Halifax for interment.

Shipwrecked at Chebucto Head

Registered in England and carrying mostly English crewmen with the exception of a few Nova Scotians, *Isleworth* netted 3,000 tons. S.S. *Isleworth*, under charter from Nova Scotia's Dominion Coal Company, left Boston on Thursday March 7, 1912, for Louisbourg. By Sunday, as she travelled farther north, *Isleworth* encountered ice. Pounding her way through drift ice, the steamer soon faced difficulty. Then, about fourteen miles from her destination, Louisbourg, three blades of her propeller snapped off, perhaps after hitting a piece of ice.

Captain Redding of Edinburgh, Scotland, told of the experience later: "This misfortune left the ship in a badly crippled condition in a field of heavy ice, with but one propeller blade to forge the heavy boat through the solid mass. We had a hard fight against big odds, but after a lot of difficulty the ship was free of the bulk of the ice. [We] were heading for Halifax intending to have a new propeller installed there. We made slow progress — less than three and a half knots an hour."

Slogging along through ice, *Isleworth* may have made Halifax. But the elements of nature are unpredictable; thus it was not the ice or heavy seas which finished off the steamer, but the age-old nemesis — fog. As Redding explained, "On Wednesday, March 13, we encountered fog as we slowly approached Chebucto Head. I thought we were yet some distance away when, with but a few seconds warning, the ship struck broadside on a ledge, only a few feet from shore. This was about five o'clock in the evening, but the fog whistle could not be heard on board *Isleworth*. The sea was pretty rough, breaking over the steamer. In a few minutes holes were rent in the ship's bottom and she began to fill with water."

Redding ordered one of the boats lowered. Its crew made five trips back and forth to the shore, a short distance away, before all were rescued. The last men off were in greatest danger, for the steamer was perched precariously on the ledge and it was feared she would roll off the rocks into deeper water. Redding realized this and had the men leave as soon as possible. No one saved any personal belongings except the clothes he wore. The captain was the last off and left behind his charts and personal effects.

On Thursday, Captain Redding went back to the site of the wreck but, as he related later, " . . . sometime between eight and ten o'clock Wednesday night she was gone, having slipped from the ledge to deep water which completely covered her. It was fortunate the disaster did not take place at night, when the chances of saving all hands would have been very slim. If it had been stormy Wednesday afternoon, it's doubtful if any of us would have been saved."

When C.H. Harvey, the Nova Scotia Marine and Fisheries agent, heard of the wreck, he dispatched the government cutter *J.L. Nelson* to Chebucto Head to bring *Isleworth*'s crew to Halifax. They arrived there Friday, March 15 and the daily papers reported, "They were warmly clad and did not look any the worse as a result of their recent experience."

On May 17, 1912, the steamer *A.W. Perry* ran into *Albert J. Lutz* (above) off Little Hope, about twelve miles from Liverpool harbour. *Albert J. Lutz*, commanded by Captain Apt, put into Shelburne to report the collision and to replace her lost mainboom and mainsail.

A.W. Perry, travelling at eleven to twelve knots in fog, struck the *Lutz* and tore off the schooner's mainboom. The steamer sped on then finally stopped to launch search boats, but did not locate the schooner in the fog. Upon impact, *Lutz* rolled over so that water entered the cabin and the crew first thought she would sink. However, she slowly came back on an even keel.

Built in Shelburne, in 1908 *Albert J. Lutz* was sold to Newfoundland interests in 1918. She capsized off Cape Broyle, Newfoundland, in June 1919 carrying a resident of Catalina down with her. (Photo courtesy Harold Simms)

Chapter 4 (1912–13)
An explained mystery

Steamship *Morien* disappears

The story begins in Nova Scotia in mid-November 1912. The *Sydney Post* speculated on the whereabouts of the Nova Scotian collier S.S. *Morien*, which had left Louisbourg for Placentia, Newfoundland, on November 16, 1912. Newfoundland's newspaper, the *Daily News* on December 3, had a column headed "The Missing Morien" which stated, "There is still no news of the missing steamer *Morien* which has not been heard of since she left Louisbourg for Placentia."

It was a voyage of two days duration. Seventeen days after she sailed, *Morien*, carrying a thousand tons of coal destined for the Reid Newfoundland Company railway terminus at Placentia, was declared lost at sea with Captain Charles M. Burchell and his crew of seventeen. A steamer of 834 tons, she was owned by Sydney interests.

Reasoned theory, wild speculation and rumours of her whereabouts ran rampant. While people speculated, ships scoured the adjacent seas for a month after *Morien* disappeared; yet relatives of the missing crew decried the futile efforts of search parties. *Lady Laurier* and *Douglas H. Thomas*, two Nova Scotian vessels, searched the Atlantic seaboard for the steamer without sighting any wreckage. Fourteen of *Morien*'s crew have been recorded: Captain C.M. Burchell of Sydney; second engineer Louis Frazer of Pictou; from Louisbourg were chief engineer F.W. Hickey (who left a wife and four small children), W. Mosher, single, Peter McMullin, married, second mate John Bagnell, who left a wife and two children; cook Charles Clemens from France; steward Charles Earle of Halifax; the home towns of J. Hazelhurst, E. Wood, C. Wood, J. Fleming, R. Martin, first mate D.J. McDonald, and three unidentified firemen were not recorded.

On December 3, several veteran sea captains ventured their opinions of *Morien*'s fate. Captain Morgan of the steamer *Kamouraska*, which left Sydney the same night as *Morien*, reported encountering a heavy storm outside the harbour and having a difficult time weathering it. Morgan thought Captain Burchell and *Morien* would have been caught in the same gale and probably went down off Nova Scotia.

One of *Morien*'s owners, John A. Young, declared publicly he was confident the missing steamer was riding safely southward somewhere on the Atlantic. According to Young, the northwest gale combined with a strong southerly current pushed the storm-disabled steamer well south. Young's confidence was reinforced by the knowledge that *Morien* had weathered severe storms in all seasons since going into the coal trade, and Captain Burchell was one of the best at adapting his vessel to adverse conditions.

Captain E. Wallace Hickey of North Sydney, who had resigned command of *Beatrice* a few months before, was to have taken charge of *Morien* after her return to Nova Scotia from Placentia. He thought it was only remotely possible she was still drifting about disabled. Most likely, he claimed, she had struck The Keys, a well-known navigational hazard off St. Mary's Bay.

This latter opinion was shared by a veteran Newfoundland master mariner, Captain Thomas Fitzpatrick of Placentia, who knew every inch of the coast in Placentia Bay. Possibly *Morien* had foundered on the lance-like Keys off St. Mary's Bay or had struck on The Nests. Located about four miles west of Distress Cove near St. Bride's in Placentia Bay, The Nests lie about nine feet under water and the sea generally breaks over the treacherous reef.

In those years, especially from 1900 to 1930, several ships met their end on Newfoundland's southern Avalon shore. On December 20, 1912, another shipwreck, S.S. *Florence*, occurred near the community of St. Shott's. This latest disaster — more visible and with survivors who told the horrifying details — drew public attention away from the missing *Morien*.

In the same month as relatives went to church to pray for the lost souls aboard *Morien*, S.S. *Florence* struck the cliffs in Mariner's Cove, east of *Morien*'s intended destination. Out of *Florence*'s total complement of twenty-five, only five made it safely to shore. The wreck commissioner from St. John's and search parties from St. Shott's and other nearby towns combed the area off southern Newfoundland, but found no sign of the sunken *Florence* nor any bodies. Bits and pieces of the crew's clothing and assorted wreckage driven up on remote beaches was all that remained of the 2,400-ton British steamer. Thus with other tragic wrecks occurring around Newfoundland's shores, the disappearance of *Morien* was forgotten and the fate of the coal carrier remained a mystery.

"After ten years the mystery was solved," declared the *Daily News* headline on October 2, 1922. The story went on to say, "After being an unsolved mystery of the deep for nearly ten years, the fate of the ill-fated S.S. *Morien* . . . has recently been cleared up."

Edward, Edmund and Philip Keefe, three fishermen of Big Barachoix, a fishing community near St. Bride's, were working in the vicinity of The Nests in early October 1922 when they made a remarkable find. All three had had their fishing lines fouled in what they knew was the rigging of a submerged ship. On another occasion a man in his small vessel brought up part of a steamer's hawser which was attached to the wreck, but the hawser could not be salvaged.

On a clear day when the water around The Nests was calm, it was possible to see the outline of the vessel lying on the bottom. Although no official dive search was conducted, nor was the wreck site ever investigated by marine authorities, local people could see a steamer's shape and knew it was the missing *Morien*. Possibly locals had pulled up identifiable items from the wreck, but were reluctant to admit it.

Fishermen of St. Bride's, Placentia, and Big Barachoix claimed the heavily laden vessel struck the rocks in the night during the mid-November storm ten years previously, filled with water and slid off into water taking her crew with her. The dire prediction of Placentia's Captain Fitzpatrick had proven correct. Remarkably, with *Morien* in such close proximity to land and inhabited harbours, no wreckage of any description and no bodies ever came ashore. Even more extraordinary was the underwater view of the missing *Morien* on the bottom near St. Bride's — a decade after she disappeared.

Wreck of the ore carrier *Glace Bay*

All hope for the salvage of the ore carrier *Glace Bay* was abandoned by May 15, 1913. *Glace Bay* left Sydney for Bell Island, Newfoundland, on the last day of April and encountered fog a few miles off the southern Avalon Peninsula. Under command of Captain Plumb, she carried a crew of forty-four; all but ten were "celestials" or Chinese sailors. By the time the ore carrier reached Mistaken Point, near Cape Race, fog was a virtual blanket forcing Plumb to reduce speed to half.

Many sea-girt areas along the Atlantic seaboard can claim the dubious distinction of "Graveyard of the Atlantic," including Sable Island, Scaterie, and the French islands of St. Pierre and Miquelon, but the southeast Avalon Peninsula has, in its own right, been known as a graveyard of wrecked and sunken ships. Fog enshrouds the land mass of Cape Race and Mistaken Point for an average of 158 days a year, reducing the effectiveness of lighthouses. An added menace along the coast is a strong tidal current which tends to carry vessels northward, too close to land.

Glace Bay first hit the fog on early Thursday morning, May 1. On Friday morning conditions were worse. The captain, who had not slept for more than twenty-four hours, was relieved on the bridge by Chief Officer Gibson. At 4:30 Friday afternoon, May 2, *Glace Bay* struck Mistaken Point. By this time, *Glace Bay* was creeping along in a fog so thick that it was impossible to see the bow of the ship from the captain's bridge.

No one on board seemed to realize the dangerous position or what had occurred until all heard a crash when the vessel struck land. Through the shroud of fog, the crew could see a high perpendicular cliff looming before them. Impact was so great some men were thrown from their bunks and slightly injured. The forward part of *Glace Bay* was ripped open and seawater rose rapidly in the hold. In less than two hours there were four fathoms of water amidships and an equal amount aft. The two engines were below water; the main steam pipe and other parts had come off their bedding or were under water.

Captain Plumb could see no other choice but to save the lives of those on board. The vessel was pounding on the rocks with a heavy sea running. Plumb ordered out three lifeboats. One of the sailors recalled how *Glace Bay* was abandoned: "Just about this time the celestial [Chinese] members of the crew began to kick up a row as they wanted to get on the boats first. . . . On reaching the shore we made fires and warmed ourselves. The next day we returned to the ship, got our belongings and rowed to Portugal Cove, a distance of seven miles or perhaps more. There we boarded the S.S. *Daliene* and were brought to St. John's."

As for the ore carrier *Glace Bay*, she remained visible for a short time, her back broken, a battered mass of scrap iron.

On May 19, 1913, the steamer *Gerald Turnbull* ran aground at Gannet Dry Ledge near Yarmouth. Such was the exposed position of the steamer that all aboard, including a number of Halifax crewmen, were in danger for their lives. A tugboat brought the news to Yarmouth that the crew had left the wreck. *Turnbull's* officers had hailed a small fishing boat and requested it take a message to Yarmouth, asking for a tug to come "Take us off, for God's sake." The little boat started for Yarmouth, met the steamer *Bridgewater*, delivered the message and then proceeded to Deep Cove. After *Bridgewater* returned the crew to land, she went back to the site and began salvage operations on the wrecked steamer.

While this is not the remains of either *Gerald Turnbull* or *Glace Bay*, it shows what the ravages of time and the relentless pounding of the sea can do to ships stranded on hostile shores. These engines, from an unknown wreck, are visible today on Seal Island, Nova Scotia. (Photo courtesy Captain Hubert Hall, Shipsearch Marine, Yarmouth)

Louisbourg schooner wrecked at Cape George

About a month after the loss of *Glace Bay*, the schooner *Maud Carter* left Louisbourg bound for Charlottetown. Heavily laden with coal, she ran afoul of the weather off Cape George, north of Antigonish. The high winds of July 7 forced the captain to run under bare poles, with no sail. About four miles off Cape George, *Maud Carter* caught a particularly strong gale and the crew battled to take down all sail. Heavy rain and pitch blackness made the situation even more trying. In the windstorm, the watch tackle broke away from the main boom leaving the schooner helpless. Relentless waves buffeted the sides and pounded the stern until timbers worked loose. With great difficulty the captain and crew launched the dory and rowed for shore near Cape George. Owned by Captain Weatherbee, *Maud Carter* was manned by Tremain Cook of Isaac's Harbour, James MacPherson from Louisbourg, and William J. Morgan of Newfoundland.

Disappearance at Bird Rocks

In November of 1913 the discovery of wreckage on the beach at Bird Rocks, a few miles north of the Magdalen Islands and about 110 miles from Sydney, strongly indicated the 3,380-ton British collier *Bridgeport* had been lost. The vessel, chartered by Dominion Coal and with a crew of forty-five, was reported overdue. The wreckage included an inside pine panel of a ship's cabin. It was painted white and had two portholes with a teak border. There was no metal attached to the board, neither did it bear any name, yet it was enough evidence that Dominion Coal officials had no doubt it was part of the hull of the missing *Bridgeport*.

Comparatively fine weather prevailed when *Bridgeport* sailed from Sydney on the Saturday afternoon of November 1. But shortly after she put to sea a terrific storm of wind and snow rolled in from the northwest. The ship would have had to contend with the full force of the elements after reaching Cape North.

Bridgeport did not arrive at her destination, Montreal, in due time. As soon as the agent of the government marine and fisheries department at Montreal learned she was unaccounted for, he dispatched Captain

Marsters and the steamer *Louisbourg*. Captain Marsters reported he had proceeded to the Gulf of St. Lawrence up as far as Fame Point, Gaspé, and investigated the coasts of Anticosti Island, the western coast of Newfoundland, and the seas off these coasts. He had avoided the usual shipping lanes; instead, he directed his attention to areas where, according to weather reports of the time, *Bridgeport* would have drifted if her engines had broken down. By November 12 Marsters concluded that if *Bridgeport* was still afloat the thorough search would have located her; thus the prospect of now finding her afloat was hopeless.

The steamer *Montcalm* had also scoured an area in the Gulf of St. Lawrence for a week beginning November 6. She had more success, locating the ship's cabin panel and other debris at Bird Rocks near the Magdalens.

Wacousta, according to a message from Montreal, had spoken to *Bridgeport* when both were sixty miles out of Sydney and bound for the St. Lawrence River. Dominion Coal officials claimed this information was false. *Wacousta* had left North Sydney twelve hours behind the missing ship and, due to the wild storm, did not make Bird Rocks until forty-eight hours later, a stretch of water that is usually covered in fifteen hours. Prevailing winds were too strong to allow *Wacousta* to navigate properly and she had to run for shelter. Thus it was concluded the ship *Wacousta* communicated with was not the *Bridgeport*.

The prevailing winds in the treacherous Gulf pile up mountainous seas. *Bridgeport*, heavily laden as she was, could not weather the gale and foundered probably around November 1. Her fate, the day and hour of her wreck, and the circumstances of her going down remain a mystery. Unlike the Nova Scotian collier *Morien*, *Bridgeport's* final resting place has never been revealed.

Mahone Bay schooner missing

Mute evidence of the fate of a wrecked vessel had been discovered on the treacherous sands of Sable Island in December 1913. Speculation was that it came from the Nova Scotia schooner *Iona W.*, unheard from for about a week. Built in 1903, *Iona W.* registered 93 tons and was owned by Jacob Ernst of Mahone Bay. One of the government steamers had been out for days searching for the missing vessel.

Upon discovery of the debris, the Sable Island Superintendent sent a telegram to Charles Harvey, the local agent of the Canadian Marine Department, reporting wreckage on the eastern end of the island. It consisted of a schooner's cabin, a barometer, a ship's compass, a barrel of fish, nets, some fish hooks, and a Norwegian fog horn. Written on the cabin inside wall was, "Wind South, June 22, 1913. Cold weather. Caribou Harbour. Waiting for bait. Angus Zwicker."

Hearing this, Harvey at once communicated with Dr. Stewart, a Member of Parliament from Mahone Bay, and asked him if it were possible to trace Zwicker's whereabouts. Dr. Stewart learned Zwicker belonged to Mahone Bay and in June had indeed been one of the crew of *Iona W.*, but Zwicker was now fishing on another vessel. Wesley Mosher, who was on the same vessel at the time, confirmed he was a shipmate of Zwicker and that Zwicker was not presently captain of *Iona W.*

From this knowledge, Harvey ascertained the wreckage belonged to *Iona W.* and she was under command of Captain John Freeman. She had left Georgetown, Prince Edward Island, early in December 1913 with a cargo of produce for Liverpool, Nova Scotia, and had been sighted battling with a gale off Whitehead. It could only be speculated that *Iona W.*, Captain John Freeman and his crew went to their doom in the storm, probably around December 7.

Chapter 5 (1913–15)
Cut down at sea

The danger of collision at sea with larger steel ships was an ever present peril for wooden schooners. On the offshore banks the wooden schooners fished or lay at anchor near sea lanes frequented by ocean-going liners. In the friendly confines of harbours like Sydney and Halifax with modern tugs to guide ships, communication aids, and standard navigation laws collisions were less common. But the high volume of traffic, human error, misjudgment of tide, wind, and fog caused several shipping accidents and loss of life even within the great seaports of Halifax and Sydney.

Collision in Sydney harbour

When the S.S. *Wabana* hit the schooner *Annie Roberts* only one of *Annie Roberts*' crew lived to tell the tale. About 3:50 p.m. on October 22, 1913, the 2,000-ton *Wabana* left the Dominion Coal pier. Her master was Captain David Reside and the vessel, under charter by the coal company, was bound for Saint John, New Brunswick, laden with coal.

It was dark by six-thirty that evening. The wind was up, but not enough to impede the progress of the powerful steamer. As *Wabana* approached the Petrie's Ledge buoy, the watch spotted a small schooner ahead on the port bow. Both of the schooner's lights — red and green —

could be seen. This made it appear as if the schooner, apparently coming into Sydney, was bearing down on the steamer. *Wabana* turned her helm to port to clear the schooner to the starboard; still both of the schooner's lights were visible. Captain Reside ordered the ship swung to port, yet according to those aboard *Wabana* the little schooner was steering an erratic course or, as they said, "wobbling about."

Wabana stopped her engines but the forward motion of the ship, which towered above the little wooden craft, drove her forward, squarely onto the bow of the schooner with a rendering crash. Although it was dark, *Wabana*'s crew sensed the schooner sank immediately but could not tell the size of the craft or exactly the point of impact. Captain Reside ordered out one of the boats, which was soon manned and swung out of the davits. It cruised around searching for the crew of the ill-fated craft and found one man, dazed but otherwise unhurt, holding on to a plank. It was the cook, John S. Bennett, the sole survivor. What schooner was this? Who else was missing? Bennett gave the details.

Annie Roberts left Sydney en route to Lamaline, Newfoundland, on the same evening as *Wabana* and, like the steamer, she was carrying coal. *Annie Roberts*, eighty tons and owned in Hermitage, Newfoundland, was crewed by men who hailed for the most part from Hermitage: Captain John Bobbett, aged 24; cook John S. Bennett; John Francis, 50, the only married crewman; John Macdonald, 30, who had a sister, Mrs. Dan Macdonald, living in North Sydney; and Arthur Coffin, a young man, (the name was later reported as Tiffin).

According to Bennett, his schooner had little chance of escape after they sighted the steamer. A southwest gale lashed the craft and Captain Bobbett had the foresail and mainsail reefed, thus she could not manoeuver well. Bennett said: "After having put to sea that afternoon, we were returning to shelter on account of the heavy weather outside. Supper was over and all hands were on deck; the skipper and I had the watch. I was lookout.

"There is very little to tell about the wreck. We saw the *Wabana* bearing down on us, apparently going full speed. We were going a good clip too and carrying all our lights. When we saw the steamer was going to be upon us, we tried to steer clear of her, but we were unable to do so and the vessels came together with a heavy crash. The *Wabana* struck us just before the foremast, and in less than three minutes the *Annie Roberts* went to the bottom. I didn't see what happened to the other four men. I was into the water when I caught one of the planks which we had been carrying on deck. One of the boats from the *Wabana* picked me up. I cannot swim and was nearly gone when they found me. It was very cold."

Wabana stayed in the area for some time and relayed the news to Mr. McAlpine, an official of Dominion Coal. Dominion Coal immediately sent the tug *Douglas H. Thomas* at full speed to render aid to any survivors and to look for bodies. *Wabana*, undamaged in the collision, returned to the pier. *Thomas* stayed until midnight but returned with no news of the missing men. Bennett left for Newfoundland on the steamship *Portia* two days later.

On October 25, Captain William Spencer of the schooner *Florence M* reported to authorities that although his vessel was carrying coal he was going to search for bodies. "After all," he said, "I knew all the crew and they were from my home town." Spencer stopped at North Sydney to get extra grappling irons and rope. Knowing the collision occurred between Petrie's Ledge and Cranberry Head, he towed the bottom in that area for several days but found nothing. The Dominion Coal steamer *Lingan* eventually located a spar and brought it to Sydney Pier.

Finally on November 11, twenty days after the fatal accident, the sea gave up a body. It drifted in near Dominion, Big Glace Bay, and was later identified as the remains of John Francis.

Back in Newfoundland the story (with a few differing details) was told and passed down through the years by poets and folksingers:

The Wreck of the *Annie Roberts*
(stanzas two, three and four as sung by Pius Power
and taken from A. Best's *Come and I Will Sing You*)

O the *Annie Roberts* left Sydney being on a Thursday night
With a crew of Newfoundlanders with spirits gay and bright;
Filled up with coal for Lamaline that evening she did sail
With her foresail and her mainsail reefed before a southwest gale.

She sailed along and all went well 'til on that fatal night
When a steamer called *Wabana* her port light hove in sight;
Being on the *Annie* she bore down and terrified her crew
And with a crash the schooner's side was quickly broke in two.

The commander of that iron ship had spun his vessel 'round
But no sign of the missing men could anywhere be found;
But one survivor from the wreck they carried him kind and well
And landed him at Sydney, the sad tale there to tell.

Glace Bay schooner given up for lost

Less than a month after this calamity in Sydney harbour, another shipping loss appeared in the local newspaper. In a sea voyage which normally could be completed in two days, the Glace Bay schooner *Ada* left Dalhousie, New Brunswick, for Prince Edward Island. It was the last day of October. By November 21, 1913, *Ada* had not shown up in any port nor had she been sighted by another vessel. Two of her five crew were identified: owner and captain John Mullins of Glace Bay and mate John Emden of New Harris, Victoria County, whose wife resided in North Sydney. The others were believed to belong to Glace Bay. Built in Port Elgin, New Brunswick, in 1896, *Ada* netted seventy-eight tons and it was Captain Mullins' second trip in her. Information from PEI confirmed she had left there with a full load of shingles.

In the same span of time — the end of October to mid-November — the Nova Scotian tug *Alexandra* was also feared lost with her crew; later she reported in at White Point, Cape North. But throughout November and its occasional storms, there was no word from the little schooner *Ada*. At North Sydney, ships entering the harbour told of wreckage, including a quantity of shingles, that had drifted ashore on the Magdalen Islands. Joseph Salter & Sons of North Sydney telegraphed the Magdalens for confirmation of the report, but up to late November had not received a reply. Finally and sadly, on December 2, *Ada* was given up for lost.

Three wrecks in one day near Louisbourg

By July 20, 1914, conflict and political turmoil in Europe erupted into World War One or, as it was commonly termed, The Great War. On June 28, 1914, Archduke Ferdinand was assassinated and, after Austria-Hungary's humiliating demands on Serbia were refused, Austria-Hungary declared war on Serbia. Other declarations of war followed and soon every major power in Europe was embroiled in conflict.

By August 1914, although Britain and thus Canada were involved, the full impact of global war had not yet reached Nova Scotia. But Nova Scotia was to play a great part, especially on the sea, in the next four years. For now ships and marine mishaps dominated the local news: three wrecks occurred in less than twenty-four hours on the east coast of Nova Scotia. Each happened within a radius of ten miles.

Cienfuegos, a 1,100-ton Cuban ship, and the American three-masted *Harold C. Beacher* grounded hard and fast on Scaterie Island. On the same day, July 18, 1914, the Norwegian steamer *Ragna* pounded to pieces on the rocks near Baleine, a short distance from Louisbourg. All three accidents were caused by the same problem — dense fog accompanied by high seas; fortunately no lives were lost. The lifesaving staff of the eastern light of Scaterie rescued *Cienfuegos*' crew, together with their personal effects. At first it seemed possible the vessel could be salvaged, for it was thought her cargo of hard pine would enable her to withstand the action of breakers.

As soon as word reached Sydney, Dominion Coal sent two tugs, *Douglas H. Thomas* and *C.M. Winch*, to the scene. The *Thomas*, with Marine Superintendent McAlpine on board, first went to the aid of the 300-ton schooner *Harold C. Beacher*. The schooner from New York, commanded by Captain Torey who had his wife aboard, had a cargo of sand destined for Dominion Iron and Steel in Sydney. Fog was so thick rescuers were unable to locate the vessel, although authorities knew she was on the shore at latitude 45 north, longitude 64 west, near Tin Cove, Scaterie. The tug made a second attempt on July 19 but sent a radio message to Sydney saying the schooner was a total wreck. Within twenty-four hours she had broken up, but the crew, including the captain and his wife, made land without undue stress.

Ragna, a thousand-ton vessel, was in ballast and bound for St. Ann's for pulpwood. *Ragna* had run into fog three days previously and lost her bearings, eventually finding a permanent resting place a mile from Baleine. She was six-and-a-half years old and carried a crew of twenty. Her holds were full of water and, according to the tug *C.M. Winch* which went to her assistance, the Norwegian ship was already a total wreck by the time the tug reached the scene.

The tug *Douglas H. Thomas* located the stranded Cuban steamer *Cienfuegos* at Point Hall, about two miles west of the Scaterie East Light.

She was laden with pitch pine from gulf ports, bound for Montreal, and had intended to call at Sydney for bunker coal. *Thomas* could not get near because of heavy seas, but stood by waiting for a break in the weather. While the tug waited, the crew of *Cienfuegos* remained on Scaterie Island until they were transported to the mainland.

On July 20, the agent for the Marine and Fisheries Department at Sydney, Vincent Mullins, declared all three ships to be "total wrecks." He also said that it must constitute a new record for marine disasters in that area: three ships within twenty-four hours in nearly the same vicinity and with no loss of life.

Not all crewmen were so lucky; this was soon made evident in the next shipping misadventure.

Mouth of Advocate Harbour, scene of disaster

For the people of Advocate Harbour, located near Parrsboro, the news of November's fighting in World War One was superseded by reports of a tragic shipwreck. On Friday, November 13, 1914, the schooner *St. Anthony* was bound from Saint John to Selma, Nova Scotia, with a general cargo. Only one survivor of the crew of five lived to tell her fate.

Mate Samuel Redmond, found floating on a spar from the schooner, related that *St. Anthony* left on Thursday for Selma but while off Advocate Harbour struck a heavy gale. With both sails torn from the rigging, the schooner drove ashore at low tide near Advocate Harbour. She was soon broken up by heavy waves on the beach. Redmond recalled that he and two others had got onto a piece of wreckage but were washed off. His two companions drowned. The mate swam to a broken spar and held on until rescued.

Those lost were Captain W.B. Gates, cook Daniel Hanlon, seaman Harry Moore of Parrsboro, and sailor McHendrick from Hillsboro. Moore's brother had drowned at Saint John in the spring of 1913 from the schooner *Abbie Keast*. J. Newton Pugsley and Captain Gates owned the 15-year-old, 99-ton *St. Anthony*. Although the schooner and cargo were insured at Saint John, *St. Anthony* was declared a total wreck. It was the worst disaster in the Cape d'Or–Advocate Harbour area in many decades.

At Parrsboro, the same storm drove the wrecked schooner *Bobs* farther up on the beach. On November 3, 1914, *Bobs* stranded at Lighthouse Bay in the Parrsboro River, obstructing navigation until the storm which claimed *St. Anthony* pushed her bottom up on land near the lighthouse.

Hiawatha explodes in Halifax harbour

The 98-ton *Hiawatha*, owned in Burin and commanded by Captain Hubert Clarke, was moored in Bedford Basin, a section of Halifax harbour, on the morning of September 10, 1915. Clarke had five crewmen with him: cook Tom Farrell, Tom Hussey, James Saunders, Fred Kirby, all from Burin, Newfoundland, plus William Hooper of Lamaline.

Built in Lunenburg as a two-masted schooner to be used in the foreign trade, *Hiawatha* had made many voyages overseas but on this trip she was scheduled to deliver gas from Halifax to Burin — 400 barrels of gasoline and 100 barrels of oil. Captain Clarke, who for years had handled and carried cargoes of this sort, was considered a careful and reliable man in the matter of fire and matches.

After loading the gasoline, Clarke awaited suitable sailing conditions. On the morning of departure, cook Tom Farrell lit the galley fire using gasoline. Flames shot up, partially burning Farrell's beard and face, catching flammable materials nearby and setting the schooner's galley afire. Clarke rushed down to help put out the fire; his clothes ignited and he jumped overboard to extinguish the flames but later died from his burns. Hooper and Saunders lost their lives. Farrell and Kirby, who broke his leg, were taken to Victoria General Hospital; only Hussey escaped uninjured.

Farrell spoke about the loss of the *Hiawatha*: "We were going to sail this morning for Newfoundland and I had gone forward in the galley to get breakfast for the boys. We had not been able to sleep in the foc'sle the night before because of the fumes from gasoline which had settled there. I went to light the fire in the stove, when suddenly there was a sharp explosion and the forecastle was a mass of flames. I leaped for the companionway and got through safely but just in the nick of time. I jumped overboard and escaped with minor injuries. Kirby who was leaning on the starboard rail, was thrown to the deck by the explosion and he, too, jumped into the water. In doing so he fractured his leg. I think Captain Clarke also jumped from the ship. It all happened so quickly, it is hard to say what each man did. Saunders and Hooper perished in the flames."

Hiawatha burned to the water's edge and stranded on a reef near the Bedford Basin pier of Imperial Oil, with her deck caved in and her ribs protruding from what was left of the hull. The fire was witnessed by the crew of a navy ship anchored close to the schooner. A report written for the Halifax papers stated: "At six-thirty a.m. the men on the warship heard an explosion and looking toward the schooner, saw a sheet of flames sweep along the deck and up the masts and rigging. Flames took full possession of the ship and it was impossible to board her. The cries of the men who had jumped overboard were heard and they were quickly brought to shore. The mate made his way to land. Thanks to the work of the oil company's tug *Togo*, the blaze did not spread to the oil storage tanks. The schooner, however, was totally destroyed."

Hiawatha's value was $5,000 and the uninsured cargo was worth about the same.

Above is the derelict *South Wind* in Yarmouth harbour. Very few ships ended their days drawn up on a beach to rest and decay peacefully. Those which became floating museums, restored and preserved in mainland ports, like *Theresa M. Connors* in Lunenburg, can be counted on one hand. A few were transferred to foreign owners and thus passed out of our knowledge. (Photo courtesy Captain Hubert Hall, Shipsearch Marine, Yarmouth)

Chapter 6 (1914–20)
Dodging bombs and storms

Nova Scotia, as part of the Dominion of Canada and its allegiance to Britain, became heavily involved in The Great War — sending troops to fight the German forces and supplying goods to war-torn European nations. German submarines exacted a terrible toll on Nova Scotian vessels.

In 1906, the German navy was one of the first to adapt the diesel engine to the submarine, providing the underwater craft with a means of strong propulsion. With the development of the periscope and the self-propelling torpedo, the submarine became a formidable factor in naval warfare. The effectiveness of the submarine was demonstrated during World War One when German subs, known as U-boats, were used extensively against Allied warships and merchant vessels. With no means of protection, the sailing schooners and unarmed steamers of Nova Scotia were easy targets for the U-boats. In spite of this, Nova Scotian ships continued to supply dried salt fish to overseas markets, returning with cargoes of salt or molasses.

Several months after the outbreak of World War One, the German war machine resorted to the submarine fleet to bring Britain to her knees. By January 1917 the Germans, convinced they could starve Britain in five months, entered into unrestricted submarine warfare, which by the summer of 1918 reached its peak in the waters off Nova Scotia. This policy,

A German World War One submarine in the Kiel Canal, in northwest Germany. German technology put their subs, or U-boats, at the forefront of military technology. In 1906, the German navy was one of the first to adapt the diesel engine to the submarine, providing the underwater craft with a means of strong propulsion. With the development of the periscope and the self-propelling torpedo, the submarine became a formidable factor in naval warfare. (Photo courtesy National Archives of the USA)

at least in its initial stages, was spectacularly effective. Allied shipping losses increased throughout the war, reaching a peak of 869,000 tons by April 1917.

Nova Scotia tern sunk by U-boat

One of the first instances of the power and terror that could be inflicted by enemy ships came early in the war. On November 1, 1914, *Wilfred M*, a tern schooner, left Lunenburg for Newfoundland to load fish destined for Bahia, Brazil. After leaving St. John's on December 19, two months passed before any news of her whereabouts came back to Nova Scotia — the accounts told of her encounter with a German warship.

Wilfred M, built in 1909 at the Smith and Rhuland yards in Lunenburg, netted 200 tons and was owned by William Duff, Howard Webb,

J.J. Kincey and others. She was commanded by Captain Cyrus Parks of Parks Creek who had two Lunenburg men — mate Sedley Young and Kenneth Iveson, the son of Captain Christian Iveson — with him, plus two or three other seamen.

Off the eastern coast of South America on January 14, 1915, the German converted cruiser *Kron Prinz Wilhelm* hove along side *Wilfred M* and demanded the crew leave the ship. Once they boarded the battleship, she shot a broad side of shells into the helpless schooner and in a short time it sank. Aboard *Kron Prinz Wilhelm* were five more crews of British vessels totalling 323 men. All were transferred to the German steamer *Holger*, and in February *Holger* landed them in Buenos Aires, Argentina, where the British consul cared for them. Word reached Nova Scotia on February 19 that the men of *Wilfred M* and the other five vessels were safe.

Lunenburg tern schooner a war casualty?

The schooner *W. Cortada*, under Captain Edwin Backman, left Lunenburg on January 11, 1915, for Ponce, Puerto Rico, with a cargo of dried and pickled fish from Zwicker and Company. The passage south generally took about two weeks and, although the weather was fine and sailing conditions favourable, no word had been heard from the vessel. By the end of the month, relatives and loved ones feared for her safety. Another schooner *W.C. McKay*, commanded by Captain Deal, had left Nova Scotia on January 26 and arrived at Ponce in nine days. That seemed to portend something tragic had befallen *W. Cortada* for she should have arrived or, if blown off course by a storm, reported before February.

Although *W. Cortada* sailed to a neutral Puerto Rico, she carried a cargo from a British port. It was the opinion of ship owners that the tern became prey to a German cruiser. *W. Cortada* was two years old, and Captain Backman one of the youngest and most progressive commanders out of Lunenburg. The three-masted, 117-foot schooner was built by Smith and Rhuland of Lunenburg in 1912. On February 8, local and provincial authorities reported this Nova Scotian vessel missing and presumed lost with crew. Sailing on *W. Cortada* were seven men, all married and from Lunenburg or the surrounding area: Captain Edwin (or Edward)

Backman, Edison Beck, mate Eleazor Beck, Gaton (or Gatend) Demone, cook Calvin Dagley, Samuel Heisler, and seaman Kenneth Meisner.

During the course of the war at sea, schooners continued to run a deadly gamut between bombs and storms. The 174-ton tern schooner *Fleetly*, out of Lunenburg, was abandoned at sea February 4, 1915. The British steamer *Mechanician*, bound for Europe, rescued the crew. *Fleetly* left Louisbourg for St. John's, but a storm drove her well off course and she ended her days 500 miles south of Sable Island. Incoming steamers reported terrific gales and heavy seas; this, combined with the intensely cold weather, loaded the schooner with ice until she was helpless.

On February 5, C.H. Harvey, the Nova Scotia Marine and Fisheries agent, received a wireless message from the *Mechanician* via Cape Race stating she had picked up the crew of *Fleetly*. *Fleetly*, owned and managed by W.N. Zwicker of Lunenburg, went to the bottom at latitude 42.46 north, longitude 51.53 west. Three of her crew were Captain Archibald Lohnes, mate Johnson and steward (or cook) Tyson of Lunenburg.

The hospital ship *Letitia*, (above) grounded in Portuguese Cove, August 1, 1917. While bringing Canadian soldiers home from the battlefields of Europe, she approached Halifax and a harbour pilot took her wheel to guide her into port. A few minutes later *Letitia's* long and distinguished career ended. (Photo courtesy Captain Hubert Hall, Shipsearch Marine, Yarmouth)

Although the greatest impact of the Halifax Explosion was felt on land, it was the result of a collision of two ships in Halifax harbour. The disaster has often been written about, thus it is not the intent here to detail the cataclysmic event. Suffice to say, during World War One convoys of ships loaded with war supplies, food and munitions gathered in Bedford Basin in preparation for the voyage across the Atlantic. They were usually accompanied by warships as an armed escort.

Early on December 6, 1917, the French munitions ship *Mont Blanc* left her anchorage outside the harbour to enter Bedford Basin. At the same time the Norwegian vessel *Imo* left the Basin bound for New York to pick up relief supplies for Belgium. At 8:45 a.m., the ships collided in the narrowest part of Halifax harbour and the resulting fire caused a tremendous explosion twenty minutes later — the world's largest man-made explosion before the atomic age and the bombing of Hiroshima. More than 1,900 people died and in excess of 9,000 were injured. Loss of homes, businesses and ships was massive.

The Norwegian vessel *Imo* lies wrecked on the Dartmouth shore after the Halifax Explosion as armed guards stand watch against looters. Seven of her crew were killed. *Mont Blanc*'s crew had abandoned ship minutes before she exploded. The Nova Scotian tug *Stella Maris*, which was next to *Mont Blanc* at the moment of explosion, was hurled out of the water and landed on shore near Pier Six. Captain Brannon and his entire fifteen-man crew died. Both *HMS Highflyer* and *HMS Niobe* suffered damage and had men killed and injured. The harbour tug *Douglas H. Thomas* was also heavily damaged, while *Rogers*, a steamer associated with a Dartmouth sugar refining company, sank with no trace of her crew.

Slowly the city of Halifax recovered from the disaster. At sea the enemy barrage intensified. By the summer of 1918, shipping roster books were filled with entries such as, "Bombed by submarine in the Atlantic," "Torpedoed off Halifax," or "Sunk by enemy sub on St. Pierre Banks." On August 25 three Lunenburg schooners — *C.M. Walters*, *E.B. Walters* and *Verna D. Adams* — were attacked, bombed and sunk. With such an array of wartime destruction of the Nova Scotian fleet, one close-up of an encounter will suffice.

When the seventeen-man crew of the Yarmouth schooner *Nelson A* arrived in Lockeport on Monday, August 5, 1918, they collectively told a dramatic story. Built in Shelburne about fifteen years before and owned by Henry A. Amiro (or Amirault) of Yarmouth, the 72-ton *Nelson A* had been fishing on the LaHave banks for two weeks and was homeward bound to Yarmouth with a load of cod and halibut.

At noon on Sunday, August 4, *Nelson A* was about eighteen miles south-southeast of Gull Rock. Captain John Simms kept watch on deck while most of the crew ate dinner or relaxed in the forecastle. Simms sighted a submarine about seven miles distant. She came up to them at full speed without firing a shot, stopped near the stern, and signalled Captain Simms to heave to. The sub commander, speaking good English, told Simms to abandon ship and "be quick about it" for he was going to sink her. The crew, some of whom had just come from the forecastle and had no coats, hats, or shoes, immediately launched four dories and jumped into them.

The story is best told in Simms' words: "He [the sub commander] also ordered us to send a dory to bring a party from the submarine aboard my schooner. We sent a dory and seven of them came aboard; all of them except two spoke English as well as I do, although they also spoke German. I asked if I might get a pair of boots. The captain, or the man I took to be captain, replied that I could, also calling for me to get our papers and flag. These I gave him.

"We then left the schooner and they set the bombs. They took our log line and hauled one end of it under the schooner's stern, making it fast to the main rigging. They then proceeded to 'keel-haul' one of their bombs. It was evidently timed as the Germans seemed in no hurry to leave the ship. The first one did not explode. They returned to the schooner and set another, which exploded in ten to twelve minutes. It blew the ballast and other material from the hold as high as the masthead and she split in two, sinking in seven minutes. None of my crew were injured."

Nelson A, which an hour or two before had been a home and workplace for seventeen men, was now gone. Fortunately the day was civil and the ocean relatively calm. In an act of compassion or sympathy, the German crew advised the Yarmouth men everything was all right and that there was another British vessel a short distance to the south. Captain Simms and his crew would have none of this advice, preferring to pull for Gull Rock. They had no provisions aboard the dories — as the submariners had ransacked the schooner for supplies, even taking the bread which the crew had left at the table — and wished to take no chances on the high seas with the enemy present. About ten o'clock that night they landed at Gull Rock.

The next day, August 5, they reached Lockeport where they told their story. That same day an auxiliary boat *McLachlan*, owned by Swim Brothers of Lockeport, was fishing twenty miles from Lockeport. She was chased by a submarine, but before the sub reached her a large steamship came in view. The "water wolf," as the seamen called her, proceeded to go after the steamer, a much larger prey. *McLachlan* arrived safely in Lockeport.

Engaging the enemy at mouth of Halifax harbour

The Imperial Oil tanker *Luca Blanca* left Halifax on August 5, 1918, bound for Mexico, armed with a single twelve-pound gun, and accompanied by another unarmed tanker. Just off the outer Halifax buoy she was struck in the stern by a torpedo. The "Hun Sea Wolf," as the crew called the U-boat, was spotted about three miles away. Both tankers turned to escape to port, which the unarmed tanker reached, but with *Luca Blanca* it was a fight to the finish.

Although badly damaged, slowly sinking by the stern and with her twelve-pounder crippled, the steamer fought a gruelling three hour battle. Sorely outclassed but undaunted, the *Luca Blanca* exchanged fire with the U-boat. Two men were killed on the after deck where they were attempt-

The Luca Blanca Going Down Off Halifax

THE above sketch is the artist's conception of the sinking of the oil tanker Luce Blanca, off Halifax harbor yesterday afternoon. Details for the sketch were furnished by a survivor. It will be observed that the tanker is sinking by the stern and the Hun U. can be observed in the left-hand corner of the sketch.

Artist's conception of the sinking of *Luca Blanca*, an oil tanker, eighteen miles southwest from the outer gas buoy off Halifax. The U-boat can be seen lurking at top left. (Taken from *Halifax Herald*, August 6, 1918)

ing to stem the inflow of water; another had his leg blown off while shells exploded on and near the tanker.

When the tanker, now ablaze amidships, began settling fast, the crew of thirty-four put off three lifeboats and rowed for the nearest shore. An American revenue cutter, alerted by a wireless SOS, reached two lifeboats while the third made land several hours later.

The presence of enemy submarines laying mines and lurking so close to Halifax harbour led many to believe the foe had a land base somewhere on Nova Scotia's shore. So prevalent was this belief, the *Halifax Herald* in its August 6, 1918, issue offered a reward of $5,000 to any person supplying information that resulted in the seizure and destruction of the "wolf hole or nest."

No base was found and the peril on the sea continued. Word from one schooner claimed that six other schooners fishing near each other were sunk on August 6. Appendix D gives the crew list of one of these, a Gloucester, Massachusetts, schooner *Muriel* manned by Nova Scotians.

The 150-ton tern schooner *Gladys J. Hollett* of Burin, Newfoundland, also encountered the enemy U-boat off Halifax on August 6. After her crew was ordered off, the schooner was shelled and she fell over on her side but did not sink. *Hollett*'s crew rowed to Sambro lighthouse and reported the incident. Within a few hours, *Gladys J. Hollett* was towed into Halifax and repaired. She then resumed her work until March 30, 1923, when she was crushed in ice off Cape Race, Newfoundland.

The signing of the Armistice Treaty on November 11, 1918, which marked the end of World War One, was a welcome relief for ship owners and sailors who had had to contend with enemy ships on the high seas. But shipwrecks caused by weather, rocks and human error continued.

Story out of Hawk Point

Gilbert Crowell of Hawk Point, near Shelburne, returned home on December 9, 1918. He had had a trying experience at sea and believed he was "lucky to be in the land of the living."

Crowell had signed on with Captain Ralph Anderson as one of six crewmen on the schooner *Alcaea*, bound from Shelburne to New York for coal. *Alcaea*, owned by Captain Charles Anderson and commanded by his son Ralph, was built in 1899. The passage down went well; at New York *Alcaea* took on 192 tons of coal and headed home.

Early in December on a Sunday morning, while twenty-four miles southwest of Cape Sable, a series of gales pummelled the schooner to such an extent both masts broke. The falling masts and spars struck the side of the schooner, smashing the lifeboats and rendering them useless. For several hours it looked as if *Alcaea* would sink as the dangling spars repeatedly pounded the side of the schooner. Eventually after much gruelling work, the crew cleared the wreckage and it floated behind the schooner. In the heavy winds the debris served as a drag to check the forward progress of the schooner.

This setback marked the beginning of trouble, for as Crowell reported: "The schooner was leaking badly. The pumps were kept going but the water in the hold gained rapidly. We made a signal by burning oakum, soaked with paraffin, but all to no purpose." The next morning, Monday, the crew placed another distress signal at the top of one of the mast stumps. Nothing happened to give any encouragement until about two p.m. when someone spotted a sail in the distance.

"It proved to be," Crowell said, "the schooner *Donald J. Cook* coming from New York with coal. She bore down and effected a rescue with the least possible delay. It was a timely rescue." And Crowell was right. A few hours later, *Alcaea*, weighted with her heavy burden of coal, went to the bottom. Her crew would have had no lifeboats and Crowell said there would have been another "mystery of the sea."

Donald J. Cook, built in the Smith and Rhuland shipyards at Lunenburg in 1918, landed the beleaguered men at Riverport. To finish his trying tale of the sea, Gilbert Crowell gave great compliments to the captain and crew of the rescue schooner. Once aboard they received the kind treatment afforded all shipwrecked sailors. Captain Anderson carried no insurance on *Alcaea* and had, not long before, refused an offer of $8,000 for her.

Yarmouth schooner in collision

The fishing vessel *Francis A.* had been in a thick fog all day on September 9, 1919. Most of the crew of twenty had spent their time on deck cleaning and dressing their catch. At six o'clock all her sails were up, flapping in a three-knot southwesterly breeze, and the vessel was bearing west at a location latitude 43.30, longitude 61.44. The crew sounded her fog horn almost continuously and sat unconcerned at their work, little knowing the fate which in a few minutes would overtake them.

Francis A., built in Shelburne in 1906, measured eighty-four feet long, twenty-two feet wide and registered ninety-three tons. She had left Yarmouth on her ill-fated trip on August 11 and had secured one of the largest catches taken that year, as it was estimated she had on board 18,000 pounds of halibut and about 70,000 of shad. Captain Ross planned for another day's fishing, which would give the vessel a record trip, after which he would return to Yarmouth.

Now her crew had to contend with a common spectre of disaster on the high seas — collision. For suddenly through the fog the men heard a steamer's whistle. Several of the crew were down in the hold and hearing the whistle scrambled up to the deck.

Through the fog, the white foam from the bow of the steamer was visible as the ship headed directly toward the schooner's port side. Seeing a collision was inevitable, the fishermen frantically launched a dory, but the dory had no sooner touched the water when the steamer crashed into

Frances A. The schooner's crew rushed to the starboard side of the craft and leaped into the sea.

The steamer did not cut the schooner in two but went in as far as the mainmast. As the sinking vessel rolled to starboard the ship passed over her. The schooner went down immediately; some of the men stated afterwards they did not see their vessel after she was hit. As *Francis A.* sank, the water was soon littered with wreckage — dories, buoys, tubs and other deck gear — which helped save fourteen of the crew.

The steamer stopped and lowered a boat to pick up those who were in the water and had been kept afloat by clinging to debris. Soon they were all safely on board and when the boat returned to the ship, the survivors, some of whom had injuries, were carefully lifted onto the steamer's deck. A quick count showed six of *Francis A*'s men were missing. Shipmates realized their young skipper, Captain Percy Ross, the man who had guided their fortunes that summer and personally cared for the well being of his crew, was not among the rescued. Captain Ross was 30 years of age and of exceptional ability as a fisherman and master of fishing vessels. He resided on Argyle Street, Yarmouth, and left a widow.

When the steamer's officers were sure the search was complete, the rescued fishermen were given dry clothes, fed, and were well cared for. Nine names of those rescued have been recorded: Edmund Harris, Fred Jacquard, Murray Goodwin, Leo Clements, Leo Porter, Lem FitzGerald, Robert Doucette, George LeBlanc, and Jack Sams. The lost were: Captain Percy Ross; his brother Ainslie Ross, 27, of Digby who left a widow and three children; Joseph Harris, 28, Comeau's Hill, survived by his wife and three children; Fred FitzGerald, 25, Comeau's Hill, single; James Gardner, 50, widower, of Argyle Sound, with an adult family; and Thomas Muise, 42, whose widow and eight children lived in Belleville.

The Pauline Lohnes sinking — Debris and wreckage float away from a schooner cut down by an ocean-going steamer. These photos were taken from the deck of the Belgian liner *Jean Jadot*, June 17, 1937, when she sliced into the fishing schooner *Pauline Lohnes*. The liner rescued the schooner's crew and took them to New York. *Pauline Lohnes*, built in Nova Scotia, was owned in 1937 by Chesley Boyce of Jersey Harbour, Newfoundland. (Photo: K. Krantz Collection, Marine Archives, St. John's)

Loss of *Belle of Burgeo* at Inner Sambro

In the fall of 1919, off Halifax harbour on the rocks of Inner Sambro, mute evidence of a shipwreck was found. Fishermen picked up pieces of wreckage: one part of a nameplate had BELLE on it, another with BURGEO. Parts of a derelict hull were located floating bottom-up while the surface of the sea around Sambro was covered with oil.

On September 8, a few days after the initial sightings, the wreckage was identified as a schooner once owned by Moulton of Burgeo, the 70-ton *Belle of Burgeo*. The schooner had left Halifax with a cargo of oil and gasoline — 350 barrels shipped by Imperial Oil to St. John's. She had been towed out of Halifax by the harbour tug and, when the tug left, *Belle of Burgeo* proceeded to sail on. The tail end of a tropical hurricane swept the Atlantic coast and had apparently pushed her onto the dangerous Sambro Ledges, rocks that had claimed many ships in the past. Farquhar and Company, the schooner's agents, valued the cargo at $5,000 and the vessel at $10,000, both insured.

There was no sign of her five crewmen. At the time of her loss she was registered to James Dunne of North Sydney, captained by John Haldane, with mate George Martin, both of Halifax, and her cook was Peter Bennett of Port aux Port, Newfoundland. Two other men who perished in

75

the shipwreck were Scandinavians, who had signed on after their own schooner, *N.T. Connelly*, was wrecked at Sable Island some weeks before.

Stanzas two to five of *The Wreck of the Belle of Burgeo*, the local poem/folksong written long ago describes the disaster:

> She sailed away from Halifax,
> For Newfoundland was bound,
> Her cargo oil and gasoline,
> A schooner staunch and sound.
> But soon a heavy gale came on,
> When reaching Sambro Shore,
> And in that gale she foundered,
> And soon she was no more.
>
> John Haddon, her commander,
> And five more seamen brave,
> That evening went down in the *Belle*
> And met a watery grave.
> Peter Bennett hailed from Newfoundland,
> As did George Martin too,
> George Johnson and Paul Manges,
> That formed the schooner's crew.
>
> They left their homes in happy glee,
> As from the pier did sail,
> Light hearted and in health and strength,
> As they leaned over the rail.
> They cast their lines that afternoon,
> And soon she sailed away,
> With mainsail and with foresail set,
> As she sailed out that day.
>
> It soon did blow a hurricane
> While seas and wind did rise,
> It was a hard and trying time
> On those poor sailor boys.
> She foundered in that fearful storm,
> And went down in that gale,
> And not one soul on board the *Belle*
> Is left to tell the tale.

In December another Nova Scotian schooner disappeared with her crew — this time farther from home. The winds of fall gave way to harsher winter storms. On December 1, 1919, lightkeepers on Isle aux Vanquers, near St. Pierre harbour, came upon a vessel aground and hard over on her starboard side. Anchors held her fast near the shore, but no sign of life could be seen. The watchman observed wreckage and debris drifting near the rocks, with three broken dories and pieces of the schooner's cargo floating nearby.

Subsequent identification of the wreck proved it was *Minnie J. Dicks* of Sydney — skippered by Captain Monroe who also had his brother aboard and three other crewmen, all from Cape Breton. From the scanty information gathered about the schooner, she had been bound for Rose Blanche laden with salt. By December 5, all five bodies had been recovered.

Fox River ship becomes mysterious derelict

To the newspapers of the day, the discovery of an abandoned Nova Scotian ship seemed like a repeat of the story of the ill-fated crew of the brig *Marie Celeste*, an unsolved nautical enigma found forty-seven years before. Now another derelict made the headlines and was dubbed "a unique and mysterious tale of the sea" equalling any fiction or tall tale told by sailors.

E — THE HALIFAX HERALD — FIRST IN

A Nova Scotia Schooner Figures in a Weird Story of the Sea : Found Abandoned With Everything in Perfect Order

The Halifax Herald of December 1, 1919, wondered if this were another sea mystery like the renown *Marie Celeste* (often mistakenly called Mary Celeste). *Marie Celeste* was launched at Spencer's Island near the head of the Bay of Fundy under the name *Amazon*. Following an accidental grounding at Cow Bay, Cape Breton, in 1868, she was repaired, renamed, and sold to American interests. In 1872 she was found drifting in relatively good order by the vessel *Del Gratia* off Gibraltar, but no one ever satisfactorily explained what had happened to Captain Briggs, his wife, infant child, and crew of seven men.

Marion G. Douglas made Nova Scotian marine history when she was found drifting and abandoned, but practically intact on November 28, 1919, near the Scilly Islands off the coast of Cornwall in the British Isles.

The next day a report relayed to Nova Scotia through the undersea transatlantic cable from London for the Montreal *Gazette* read "Nova Scotia Schooner Figures in a Weird Story of the Sea: Found Abandoned With Everything in Perfect Order." To the Scilly Islanders of Brighter Island, who happened upon the abandoned *Marion G. Douglas*, it was both a mystery and a godsend.

One report out of England said: "A strange story of the sea comes from the Scilly Islands. Soon after daybreak November 28, a three-master fore and aft rigged schooner was seen north of the islands near Shipman Head, Brighter Island. By her behaviour, she was in difficulty and was probably a derelict. The latter was found to be the case and on boarding her the Brighter men were astonished to find that every member of the schooner's crew had left. Everything was in perfect order and the ship was in no way damaged! All the sails were furled and all boats were aboard, including a smart motor launch. What had happened to the crew? What caused them to leave the ship?"

What was more amazing, as the story is told, the derelict had in her holds a cargo of wood, thus there could have been no danger of the mysterious ship quickly sinking. Her name was clearly visible on her stern: *Marion G. Douglas*. Lloyd's Registry of Shipping revealed she was built at Fox River, Nova Scotia, in 1917 and was registered to W.N. Reinhardt of LaHave.

All in all, a riddle of the sea — an abandoned ship in good working order and no trace of her crew, but there was no doubt of her worth in cash to the salvors. There would be a considerable amount of salvage money to be divided among the Brighter men.

Then just as suddenly as the mystery unfolded, the answer came — on December 2 Captain Sydney Corkum and the crew of *Marion G. Douglas* arrived in Halifax.

To Corkum, the mystery was not as great as the British papers made it to be. All was not in good order on the schooner; indeed the crew believed their lives were in imminent danger when they stepped off the derelict *Marion G. Douglas* on November 14.

According to the captain's story, *Marion G. Douglas* — manned by Captain Corkum and his crew of mate Bernard Schmeisser, cook Eben Shankle, Edward Croft, all of LaHave, J. Huey and Maurice Cross of Mount Pleasant, and Max Henson of West Berlin — left Quebec on October 6. She sailed for Scotland with a cargo of lumber deals.

From the beginning Corkum and his ship ran into foul weather. Off the coast of Ireland they encountered a southeasterly hurricane. Corkum hove his ship to, double-reefed the mainsail and took in the foresail. For five days mountainous seas buffeted *Marion G. Douglas* and swept the deck clean of anything moveable. To make matters worse, when the schooner sprang a leak the gasoline pump soon gave out from overuse. Corkum and his six men, pumping by hand with superhuman energy day and night, tried to keep the ship free of water. When the hurricane finally passed, seven feet of water filled the hold. After her crew's heroic labours, *Marion G. Douglas* was partially cleared of water and the crew hoped to reach a port.

Again the vessel was accosted by successive storms. The crew jettisoned the deckload of lumber and lightened the schooner in every possible way. As if to seal the fate of the labouring sailors, the steering gear, already seriously damaged, ceased to function totally and the schooner drifted helplessly at the mercy of the storm. The crew tried to rig up new sails, only to find the increased strain on the masts caused the ship to leak more.

Overwhelmed by this final calamity, the captain decided that with his vessel rapidly becoming waterlogged and the steering gear disabled, it was time to abandon ship. The crew had no choice. On November 14 *Marion G. Douglas* was left abandoned 160 miles off the English coast. That day the seven Nova Scotian men watched the horizon for a passing ship. Then a steamer came into sight, eventually stopped near the wallowing wreck and rescued the crew. It was S.S. *Suffolk* bound from Australia to Halifax. First the *Suffolk* stopped in Botwood, Newfoundland, to pick up cargo and arrived in Halifax December 2.

Two weeks after *Marion G. Douglas* was abandoned, she drifted near the Scilly Islands where she was towed into anchorage. Not knowing what had happened, the islanders immediate concerns were: where was the crew? Safe or lost? Why was the ship deserted while in relatively good shape? Is this a case like the unsolved mystery of the derelict *Marie Ce-*

leste? But unlike the crew and passengers of *Marie Celeste*, who were never seen again, the men of the *Marion G. Douglas* were, by this time, safely aboard the *Suffolk* and on their way to North America.

At LaHave, there must have been mixed emotions when news from the English insurer and the claims from salvage companies arrived. Owner Reinhardt was delighted to know his valuable foreign-going vessel had been found intact; the cost to build her was estimated at $90,000. As soon as Reinhardt made a cash settlement for salvage claims, he sent U.E. Woemer to the Scilly Islands to pay the bills and to bring the *Marion G. Douglas* to her home port.

Ironically, in 1927 the same vessel was found abandoned again — this time in the Pacific Ocean. By then she was owned in the United States and had been renamed *Cynthia J. Griffin*. Eventually she passed out of the records of shipping lists; her final fate is obscure.

Scaterie wreck

In the era of the Nova Scotian coal trade, the people of Main-à-Dieu, "Hand of God," were accustomed to the sight of Dominion Coal Company colliers passing by their shore. Most ships passed through Main-à-Dieu Passage without incident, but occasionally strandings and wrecks were the order of the day. On March 8 of 1920 observers from Long Point, near Main-à-Dieu, were trying to determine which steamer had run aground at Red Rocks on the southeast point of Scaterie Island.

Fears surfaced that it might be Dominion Coal's S.S. *Cape Breton*, a 1,100-ton collier. In company with *Nevada*, she had left Halifax for Louisbourg a day or so before but *Cape Breton* had not arrived at her intended destination. If *Cape Breton* had wrecked on Scaterie, people knew the vessel couldn't send a distress call as she carried no radio. To increase concern, watchers from Long Point on the Main-à-Dieu shoreline could distinguish identifying marks: the ship resembled the carrier's size and shape plus it had the company symbol, a black diamond crest, on her funnel.

The ship was first observed by fishermen gathered at Long Shore near Scaterie. They saw her drift toward Scaterie, erratic in her course and seemingly a plaything tossed by gale force winds. When she grounded, heavy seas and ice floes crashed against her and those who watched from the mainland knew she could not withstand the terrible pounding for any length of time. By dark her funnel and spars were still standing.

Apparently the ship went ashore at ten a.m. on March 7 at an isolated and exposed position on Scaterie, out of sight of the island's West Point light. The Scaterie lifesaving station was situated on the far side of the island; thus attendants there were not aware of the ship's predicament.

Drift ice in the passage had broken the undersea telegraph cable between Scaterie and the Cape Breton mainland. Heavy ice floes prevented boats from crossing the strait and authorities were delayed in determining the exact identity or condition of the stranded ship. No one from Main-à-Dieu or Long Shore could get to the site. Fears of loss of life pervaded, for there had been no movement of small boats or lifeboats which would indicate survivors.

Throughout March 8 heavy seas pounded against the wreck. The Newfoundland steamer *Kyle* left North Sydney to give assistance that evening and reached a point near the wreck at ten o'clock. Due to ice, darkness, wind, and rough weather, *Kyle* returned to port unable to help. Conditions on March 9 were no better at the wreck site: wind, which had abated during the night, freshened by daylight; waves pounded over the ice-encrusted derelict which had slipped lower in the water. Her distance from shore was judged to be a hundred yards. *Kyle* returned and stood by at the edge of the half-mile ice field that surrounded the wreck and Scaterie Island.

That day it was confirmed the stranded vessel was S.S. *Cape Breton*, now coated with ice and lying broadside, barely visible, on the rocks off Scaterie. There was no sign of her crew, believed to be about thirty men, and all were assumed lost. Her captain, John Willett of Sydney resided at Dominion Street, Whitney Pier. Because several men had signed on at Louisbourg a day or so before her departure, an accurate crew list was not available, but some of those believed to be on *Cape Breton* were: John Gillard, 21 of Harbour Grace, Newfoundland; Ernest Boudrot, 22, Poulamond; George Willett, Louisbourg; engineer John Sommers, Halifax; and mate Plynn.

The gale at Scaterie and vicinity also lashed other parts of Nova Scotia. A 55-mile-an-hour wind was recorded at Halifax but no damage to property was reported. The Norwegian steamer *Henrik Lund* dragged her anchors and went aground on the Woodside shore at Dartmouth. Winds reached seventy miles an hour at Liverpool and the chimney of Trinity Church had fallen through the roof, while lobster fishermen at Yarmouth reported damage to gear. A steamer, *Northland*, with many passengers and a full cargo of freight sheltered at Yarmouth. *Ellithrop*, an American steamer reported drifting helplessly in the gale near Sable Island, barely clearing the western bar, while the US carrier *Wisconsin*, disabled off Cape Race, was taken in tow by another American ship. Another American steamer *Guilford*, bound from Norfolk to Boston, had to be abandoned at sea. Her captain and crew survived. A devastating weekend on the Atlantic seaboard, culminating in the loss of the Nova Scotian coal carrier *Cape Breton* and her crew.

On August 13, 1920, the steamer *Martara* grounded at Gooseberry Cove, five miles from Louisbourg. Owned in New York and registered at 2,500 tons, *Martara*, in her time, had made history. For thirty years she plied between San Francisco and Alaska. Many a prospector and fortune seeker she carried north to Alaska during the Gold Rush of the late 1890s. Several episodes of gambling, fighting and threats transpired on her aged decks.

Now the steamer, bound in ballast from Philadelphia to Botwood, Newfoundland, passed Nova Scotian shores. Reports confirmed that dense fog combined with tricky currents between Gabarus Bay and Scaterie to put the old tramp steamer near shore. *Martara* had broken in two across the ledge where she had pushed her nose during the fog. With her inner and outer plates ripped to pieces by the razor-like rocks, she soon filled with water. Captain Bangs and his crew, thirty-three in total, took to her boats and arrived in Louisbourg without incident. All were Americans except her third officer, Taylor, who belonged to Halifax.

Charles A. Ritcey

Charles A. Ritcey, bound to Lunenburg in ballast from Spain, encountered a strong northeast gale with a heavy sea and the vessel was sailing under close-hauled sail. A strong current was also running to the westward.

Immediately after the ship struck Rose Head, the seven men — four belonged to Lunenburg County and three to Barbados — on board prepared to reach land. The steward tied a rope around his waist and swam to shore. When the rope was fastened ashore, the others made land on the lifeline. Captain Acker, aged 27 and unmarried, was the last to leave the vessel. As he was about to do so, the schooner, which was pounding heavily, gave a lurch and his shipmates on land did not see him again. It is presumed that the rope parted and the captain fell overboard losing his life in the breakers.

Built at Meteghan in 1917, the 360-net-ton *Charles A. Ritcey*, owned by Colin Ritcey

On September 15, 1920, the tern schooner *Charles A. Ritcey* was wrecked while attempting to enter Lunenburg harbour. Captain Oden Acker of Mahone Bay lost his life when the vessel struck Rose Head, near the entrance to the harbour. (Photo postcard courtesy of Jack Keeping)

of Lunenburg, was insured by Dale and Company of Halifax for $55,000. A few days later, Captains Silver, Corkum, and Rhuland made a survey of the vessel. By then she was high and dry on the beach and they were able to walk aboard. The spars were adrift and one side of the vessel was stove in.

Chapter 7 (1920–23)
Forest fire causes wreck?

Built at Hantsport, abandoned in the Atlantic

She was one of the largest schooners built in Nova Scotia, but *Margaret F. Dick* succumbed to Atlantic storms just two years after her launching. Porter Brothers of Halifax built the four-masted schooner in Hantsport in 1918. She had a net tonnage of 989, but her dead weight capacity was 1,500 tons. Porter Brothers sold her to the British Colony and Transportation Company, who in turn sold her to American interests operating out of Nova Scotia.

In mid-September 1920 *Margaret F. Dick* loaded salt at Ibiza, a Spanish seaport. On September 26 she stopped at Madeira Island to have the auxiliary engine repaired and on October 1 continued her journey to Lunenburg and Campbellton.

Within a couple of weeks she should have arrived at Lunenburg, but the month of October passed and she had not reported. Her failure to appear caused much anxiety and relatives of the crew looked for word of her day by day. It was intended that when she arrived in Lunenburg, *Margaret F. Dick* was to be hauled out on the newly built Lunenburg marine slipway, designed to accommodate ships of a thousand tons or more.

Managers of the new facility eagerly looked forward to giving the slipway a trial run with the four-master as a first test.

Sailing and managing a four-masted schooner on the overseas dried fish and salt run required a larger crew than what was needed on a smaller schooner. Fourteen men sailed with Captain Marshall O'Hara: mate Clarence O'Hara, the captain's brother, a resident of Isaac's Harbour; second mate Tupper Davidson, E.B. Davidson, A.S. Cooke, all of Isaac's Harbour; cook Daniel Thomas, Halifax; Arthur Mason, Liverpool; William Grant, Pictou; W. Nickerson, Clarke's Harbour; Charlie Stewart, Dover; three deckhands from Bay of Islands, Newfoundland, Arthur Madore, Walter Gallant and Arthur Ogden. Sydney Allen hailed from England.

When *Margaret F. Dick* reached latitude 41.40 north, longitude 53.42 west, a point about 400 miles southeast of Halifax, she was in a sinking condition. The dead weight of salt had opened her seams and her pumps clogged with brine from the melting salt. The crew signalled a passing ship. East-bound *Leersum* plucked the fourteen sailors from the sinking vessel and landed them at Amsterdam. Before he left the abandoned schooner, Captain O'Hara ordered her set afire so that she would not to be a menace to navigation.

The message of the salvation of *Margaret F. Dick*'s crew came via *Leersum*, across the Atlantic. The first knowledge of her loss arrived November 24, 1920, when the wife of the captain, residing in Halifax on Allan Street, received a telegram saying that *Margaret F. Dick* had been abandoned at sea and her crew picked up by a steamer. The message came from Captain Marshall O'Hara.

Preceptor at Marie Joseph Shoals

On November 27, 1920, the schooner *Preceptor* and Captain George Lee left Spaniard's Bay, Newfoundland, in ballast and soon met a typical December storm which stripped her of her mainsail and foresail. On the twelfth storm-tossed day, the crew sighted land, which they presumed to be Nova Scotia. Out of control, *Preceptor* eventually grounded on a small island. The six-man crew took to their dory, still not knowing exactly where they were. In the distance stood a lighthouse on a small island; the keepers of the light directed them to the little town of Marie Joseph, Guysborough County. Battered by waves on a lonely outcrop of rock, *Pre-*

ceptor quickly broke up. After insurance representatives visited the wreck and questioned the crew, the schooner was pronounced a total loss to her owner G.& A. Buffett of Grand Bank, Newfoundland.

Forest fire smoke from Neil's Harbour

Early Friday morning on July 29, 1921, the steamer *Volunda* went ashore at Neil's Harbour. This 1,056-ton ship out of Pictou was full of coal and became a great financial loss for the Nova Scotia Steel and Coal Company which managed her.

Volunda, bound from North Sydney to Montreal, was off course and too near the coast. As far as authorities could determine two factors caused her wreck. Exceptionally strong tides, estimated to be running at around four to five knots, may have diverted the steamer from her course and pushed her onto the rocky environs near Neil's Harbour.

Secondly, according to a report in the *Sydney Post* of July 30, 1921, the steamer miscalculated her position owing to the dense smoke from a forest fire raging around Neil's Harbour and New Haven. The drifting smoke, which hung over the sea, confused the man on watch at *Volunda*'s wheel. Running at full speed the ship passed within 200 feet of the Neil's Harbour lighthouse when she grounded. There was some disagreement over the statement that "smoke from the Neil's Harbour forest fire" caused the wreck. According to some witnesses, the smoke had subsided making it possible to see, from at least a mile away, not only the lighthouse but also the lights from ships in the harbour.

Whatever the cause, the assessment of the wreck by Vincent Mullins, an agent for Marine and Fisheries, indicated the doom of a fine vessel. His message read, "*Volunda* is thumping heavily on the rocks and taking on water." By the next day, July 31, Captain Yorke of the S.S. *Aspy* and the captain of S.S. *Douglas H. Thomas*, standing by to tow her off if possible, both agreed *Volunda* could not be freed.

On Monday, August 1, a survey team — P.W. Wilson, a representative of Lloyds Insurance, Frank Porter of Atlantic Salvage, Captain A.E. Taylor of Maritime Wrecking, D.G. McAlpine of Dominion Coal, and diver George Robinson — completed their investigation of the wreck. Weather conditions were not favourable for an extensive examination, but the diver reported that *Volunda*'s bow to midsection had been seriously damaged. From midship to the stern there was five feet of water in her holds. The rocky ledge on which she rested certainly looked unfavourable for getting the ship off even if she were lightened.

The Neil's Harbour agent for Lloyds, Reuben Payne, reported: "*Volunda* near lighthouse and full of water, deckhouse gutted, seas breaking over ship. On Monday [August 1] crew had to leave with great combers rolling over bulwarks."

The investigators, who had gone to New Campbellton and then motored to the Neil's Harbour wreck site, concluded it was best to salvage and sell the coal and ship's fittings first and then to auction the wreck. The real value was a quarter of a million dollars, but Nova Scotia Coal and Steel received very little. *Volunda* was lying in a precarious position, exposed to the full sweep of the Atlantic. No one would venture into her holds knowing that a storm or a heavy swell could send her into deeper water at a moment's notice.

The twisted wreck, devoid of winches, deck gear, stores, and supplies was auctioned off at North Sydney and went to Harry (Harris) Elman for $335: the ship for $300 and 2,500 tons of coal for $35. According to reports, one of *Volunda*'s motor lifeboats, which was still intact on deck, was worth more than what Elman had paid for the entire ship and cargo. By August 10, Elman had hired a large crew of men to remove the wireless apparatus, the valuable portions of her equipment, and to begin salvaging coal.

Wreck of LaHave schooner *Innovation*

On Thursday, July 28, 1921, the shipwrecked men of the LaHave schooner *Innovation* arrived at Halifax. They had seen their fine tern schooner go down the previous Tuesday. *Innovation*, bound to Halifax, left Little Bras d'Or on July 23 with more than 300 tons of coal consigned for Nova Scotia Steel and Coal.

When she left Little Bras d'Or the wind was light and the seas smooth. By Monday, Captain Randall stated, the crew battled a strong southwest wind with a cross sea. *Innovation* sprang a leak that could not be repaired and at four o'clock Tuesday morning, the crew abandoned the sinking ship, now wallowing and unmanageable.

The captain told of the abandonment: "We saved only part of our belongings. It was blowing a stiff wind from the southwest with a heavy sea. [We] had a motorboat and our position, after getting clear of the ship, was thirty miles southeast of Canso. We decided to make for there. Progress was slow on account of wind and sea, but later the wind moderated and better time was made. When the fog lifted, we sighted Green Island and then headed for Canso. We arrived ten o'clock that night."

Built by Leary Brothers at Dayspring in 1919 for Captain Randall, *Innovation* was managed by Frazer Gray of LaHave. When she sank, her crew was captain and part owner Morris H. Randall, mate Arthur Himmelman, steward or cook Starrat Corkum, and seamen William Boxill, Bernard Richard and Edmund Corkum She was well known in Halifax and had loaded there many times. On her maiden voyage in May 1919, she sailed on a transatlantic voyage to London carrying a cargo of syrup and sugar from H.R. Silver Ltd.

On July 29, *Rupert K*, a tern schooner, sailed en route from New Campbellton, Cape Breton, to Campbellton, New Brunswick. She caught fire in the Gulf of St. Lawrence at 48.10 north latitude, 64.10 west longitude and sank. The crew was safely landed at Grand Anse, New Brunswick. Built at Spencer's Island in 1920, the 378-ton *Rupert K* was owned by A.O. Seaman and others of Parrsboro. Her captain, John J. Taylor, also hailed from Parrsboro.

Shipwrecked crew reach St. Esprit

Captain Daniel Harris and his ten crewmen reached the Nova Scotian coast near St. Esprit after their ship *Musquash*, a sea-going tugboat out of Halifax, sank.

Owned by J.P. Porter of Atlantic Salvage and Towing, *Musquash* was a powerful tug for her size and for years had figured in many long distance tows. During the First World War she crossed the Atlantic from Halifax to England while in the service of the British Admiralty. *Musquash* had been built in Portsmouth, England, in 1894 but her first owner in Canada was Walter Stevens of Chatham. She had worked for the Allan steamship line in Saint John, New Brunswick. When *City of Columbo* wrecked at Digby, *Musquash* helped salvage her valuable cargo. Her most recent work had been towing the steamer *Basaan* from Halifax to Parrsboro, at the head of Bay of Fundy.

Musquash left Halifax for Louisbourg in early August 1921. At Louisbourg she put a line on a derrick, probably on a barge, intending to tow it back to Halifax. On the night of August 4, her Louisbourg-to-Halifax task went well until *Musquash* reached the coast off St. Esprit. The towing hawser broke and the tug returned to the derrick to reattach the line. In the heavy sea a piece of the high derrick punched a hole in the old tug's side. Within a few minutes she was going down. *Musquash*'s crew barely had time to throw off the lifeboat and saved no personal belongings. They landed on the shoreline near St. Esprit, a town located between Fourchu and Point Michaud on Cape Breton's east coast.

Thrum Cap Shoals

Before the month of August 1921 had ended, another major shipping casualty happened at Thrum Cap, treacherous ledges at the entrance to Halifax harbour.

Carrying a general cargo, mainly food, the steamer *Lady of Gaspé*, grounded at Thrum Cap, five miles below George's Island and two and a half miles from Maugher's Beach light. Oddly, Captain Neil Nicolsen attempted to navigate his large ship into the harbour without a pilot. About six p.m. in dense fog *Lady of Gaspé* struck the cap.

She had left Boston three days before, intending to stop at Halifax then proceeding to Grand Bank and St. John's, Newfoundland, with a freight of barrelled beef, flour, meal, and other food. The captain claimed: "Thick fog was on us all the way from Boston and we had to pick our way right up to the time the ship struck. I knew I was well inside of Sambro, but I couldn't hear the bell on Thrum Cap. Although it was not my watch, I remained on deck keeping a lookout with Chief Officer Wesley Munroe and Third Officer Joseph McDonald on the bridge. It was during this watch that our ship struck. We had passed the lightship buoy and were heading northwest."

Lady of Gaspé was then, Nicolsen said, running at half speed. When she ground to a standstill on Thrum Cap, the crew still could not hear the bell.

Lady of Gaspé, an iron ship owned by Nova Scotia Steamship Ltd., was launched in England in 1877. She was 229 feet long, thirty-one feet wide and registered at 770 tons. This old weary freighter had not been fitted with a wireless, thus no SOS could be sent out. The captain had to launch a boat and send a crew into Halifax to ask for assistance. They reached Campbell's wharf at 9:15 p.m., about three hours after she struck. Two harbour tugs immediately put out; while headed to the wreck, they met the captain and the rest of the twenty-four crewmen rowing for land near Maugher's Beach.

Two stranded: *Linda Pardy, Defender*

On October 31, 1921, the banker *Linda Pardy* drove ashore at Mira Gut near Sydney, while under the command of Captain Mullins of Harbour Breton, Newfoundland. The 69-ton *Linda Pardy* was originally owned in Grand Bank by Simeon Tibbo, who later sold her to Mullins with shares held by Salter's Ltd. of North Sydney. While trying to make North Sydney, she encountered heavy winds and anchored off False Bay Beach. Her anchors dragged and the schooner was driven upon the beach.

One month later on December 29, *Defender*, a 100-ton schooner captained by Leo Keeping, went ashore at Petrie's Ledge near Sydney harbour. She had left Halifax for Port aux Basques a few days previously, but heavy weather opened her seams and forced Keeping to make for North Sydney for repairs. Keeping had paid $12,000 for *Defender* two years before and had her insured for $7,000.

Barrington schooner: another victim of Thrum Cap

When reports first filtered into Halifax, it was thought the 32-ton schooner *Newhome*, breaking up on Thrum Cap shoals on November 16, 1921, was lost with crew. But unknown to those viewing the wreck, Captain Raymond Wilson and his crew of two, Isaac Kendrick and I.J. Connell, all of Barrington, had rowed to shore at the light station on Maugher's Beach. They had left Montague laden with produce — 1,000 bushels of potatoes, 100 bushels of oats and 200 bushels of turnip — all insured in PEI.

Newhome's voyage from Prince Edward Island to Barrington, which should have been completed in two or three days, had been fraught with problems from the outset. While running through the Strait of Canso she met with heavy gales and, while going past Port Hawkesbury, broke her main boom. A storm off Halifax on November 15 helped Captain Wilson decide to put into Halifax that evening for shelter. Although he had a new compass aboard, it was not working and this, according to the captain, caused the accident. Although Wilson, Kendrick and Connell were on deck watching and listening, the schooner went ashore. Wilson said, "I was not steering at the time, but had given the proper course and it was adhered to. I'm positive of this as I was on deck."

Nature's elements, thick weather, rain, rough seas put an end to *Newhome*. She grounded at midnight on November 15-16. It took the three men about half an hour to launch a dory to leave the schooner, which by then was rolling to such an extent there was a danger of her turning turtle at any moment. Then the men had a three mile row in choppy seas before they reached the safety of Maugher's Beach.

The steamer *Alfreda* brought *Newhome's* crew to Halifax where they were lodged in the Sailor's Home. No one saved any clothing or personal effects except what each man wore. Pounded by the waves on Thrum Cap, the Barrington vessel and her cargo of food and winter supplies soon became debris along the shore. The captain carried no insurance on his schooner, valued at $2,000.

Not all Nova Scotian losses at sea occurred near home, for her ships sailed to major seaports all along the Atlantic coast and beyond. On April 5, 1922, word came via the French islands of St. Pierre and Miquelon that ice had crushed a Sydney schooner.

When Captain John Petite arrived back in North Sydney he related how his schooner, *Elizabeth D*, had been caught in ice and foundered off St. Pierre. This two-masted ship, registered to F.A. Crowell of Sydney, netted eighty tons and was manned by a crew of five Newfoundlanders.

Elizabeth D, valued at $10,000 and insured for that amount, plied the coasting trade in the winter of 1921-22.

Bound from Belleoram, Newfoundland, to Halifax with a cargo of frozen herring, *Elizabeth D* had beaten her way through ice packs from Belleoram to the French islands, but there she became jammed. For several days she remained held in the floes off St. Pierre; each hour she inched closer to land. Finally a strong wind from the south pushed her on beam ends into shallow water. Once there her hull began to cave and split from ice pressure. The crew left *Elizabeth D* when all hope of saving her had been abandoned. They reached shore by walking over the ice floes.

Missing men brought to Pleasantville on LaHave's *Coral Spray*

The news, all too common and tragic, was devastating — "Cape Breton Fishermen Lost" reported the *Sydney Post* on June 27, 1922. An American schooner, *Puritan*, had wrecked on Sable Island and those missing and presumed drowned — including six Nova Scotians — were listed.

Puritan, a Gloucester, Massachusetts, fishing schooner designed and built to race Nova Scotia's *Bluenose*, struck the Northwest Bar of Sable Island on Friday night, June 23, 1922. All night the heavy seas swept over the vessel, aground on a sandy bar off the island, forcing the crew of twenty-three into the rigging to save their lives. At daylight they made their escape in two dories. But one dory upset in the surf, throwing its occupants into the water. Christopher Johnson of Newfoundland drowned within sight of his comrades. Captain Jeffrey Thomas, a native Nova Scotian, with seven men breached the breakers on Sable Island and made land.

The other sixteen rowed to the north of the island and spent the night on the ocean without food or water. *Coral Spray*, a schooner out of LaHave returning home from the fishing banks, saw them and brought them to Pleasantville, Lunenburg County, Saturday evening, June 24. Several of *Puritan*'s men who sailed into Pleasantville were originally from Nova Scotia but now resided in Gloucester: Captain Thomas, aged 47, born in Arichat, Cape Breton, but living in Gloucester; Thomas Dolorey, 62, West Arichat; Edward H. Surrett, 28, Emil Leblanc, 41, Eleasor A.

Moro, 40, and Anthony U. Burke, all originally from Tusket Hill, Yarmouth County.

The eight shipwrecked seamen who reached Sable Island walked several miles to the nearest manned lighthouse, where they were cared for by Superintendent Henry. Immediately he contacted authorities to say eight had made land and the others could not be accounted for. Henry arranged for an American ship to pick up the men. About the same time as *Coral Spray* docked in Pleasantville, the US cutter *Tampa Bay* had searched the Middle Ground, a fishing bank, for victims or survivors but found nothing. She then steamed to rescue those stranded on Sable Island and left for Halifax.

At Halifax Captain Thomas, before he knew the fate of other crewmen, described the wreck: "*Puritan* piled on the sands about two miles north of the northwest station on Sable Island. With her enormous momentum she ploughed through the bar for a considerable distance and for a brief moment it was thought she might work her way through to deep water beyond. But only for a moment, as she slowly came to stop huge seas hurling aboard sweeping her fore and aft and sealing her doom. It was in the midst of this welter of seas, breaking for a distance of five miles in a northerly direction from the northwest light, that [we] launched our dories and attempted to gain deep water . . . All hands left ship in dories, having much trouble keeping dories upright on account of sea. I saw one dory capsize, but I'm uncertain whether or not her crew was picked up by shipmates." Captain Thomas later learned the others, with the exception of one man (Christopher Johnson of Newfoundland) had been rescued by *Coral Spray*.

In the 1930s the LaHave banker *Coral Spray*, built in LaHave River in 1919, was sold to Newfoundland interests. She was a large banker at 127 net tons and 100 feet long. Her new owners, J.B. Patten and Sons of Grand Bank, put the schooner to work transporting supplies between Newfoundland and mainland Canada when the fishing season ended. In September 1937, *Coral Spray* was commissioned to carry coal from Sydney, Nova Scotia, to Lewisporte, Notre Dame Bay. On September 15 she hit rocks near St. Shott's, Newfoundland, and was wrecked. One man, Sydney Weymouth of Grand Bank, lost his life.

En route to Sydney

The headlines read, "Crew of Eight Reach Shore In Basket After Battle With Wind And Wave And Flying Spume — Shipwrecked Sailors Cared For By Kindly Fisher-Folk Of Scaterie Island." (*Sydney Post*, October 3, 1923.)

Inhabitants of Scaterie once again came to the rescue when the French steamer *Yport*, bound from Nassau to Sydney in ballast, piled on the rocks of the south side of Scaterie Island.

Yport, feeling her way along the coast during a heavy gale in late September 1923, touched a ledge. Instantly she took on water. For hours Captain Balier, his officers and crew of eight clung to the surging, tossing wreck and finally succeeded in getting a line ashore. They reached land in a crude breeches buoy — a lifebuoy or board suspended from a rope which has canvas breeches for the user's legs. This journey from ship to shore was hazardous since for the greater part of the distance the occupants of the frail basket were submerged in the boiling, roaring seas and flying spray. However, each succeeded in landing on the rocks where the Scaterie families took care of them.

Drawing of a breeches buoy similar to that which rescued *Yport*'s crew. Although such rescue devices helped save the lives of many sailors, it had its limitations: often the wreck was too far from the shore; some strandings occurred in remote, inaccessible areas; cold and weakened survivors on the wrecked ship sometimes lacked the strength to fasten, get into or hold onto the bosun's chair while being pulled to shore. (Artist: Andrea Hatch)

Yport hit on one of the most desolate and exposed points on Scaterie. The tremendous seas which battered the coast for two days made short work of the hulk. It was driven far inshore and not even the hull could be salvaged. *Yport*, owned in France, had steamed for Sydney to take on bunker coal. The French consul in North Sydney at the time, Monsieur Lacroix, made arrangements and had the crew accommodated at North Sydney.

The storm that wrecked the French vessel *Yport* on Scaterie Island on September 30, 1923, also claimed the lives of Captain Angus Richards and an unidentified man of LaHave on *Governor Parr*. This four-masted schooner had been built in Parrsboro in 1918. About mid-September, the lumber-laden *Governor Parr* was towed out of Ingramport, Nova Scotia, headed for Buenos Aires, Argentina. About 700 miles off New York, *Governor Parr* battled high winds and waves which heavily damaged her. In the storm both men were washed overboard. Richards, about 57 years of age, was a widower with grown children. After *Governor Parr*'s crew was taken off by a steamer on October 2, 1923, she was left abandoned and a derelict in the North Atlantic.

Vera B — heroism at Cheticamp

The owners' quests for cargoes and work for their schooners took the little vessels to many ports along the eastern seaboard. In the fall of 1923, the 60-ton *Vera B* sailed from North Sydney for the Magdalen Islands in the Gulf of St. Lawrence with a cargo of coal. Her captain and owner, Hezekiah Gillard, had with him two men from his home town of Fortune, Newfoundland, mate Saul Mosher, and cook Hedley Snook, while seaman John Warren hailed from St. Barbe. *Vera B* was built in Wesleyville, Bonavista Bay, in 1914.

On October 23, the vessel met with a wild storm and Gillard decided to make for Cheticamp or some other haven in Nova Scotia or Prince Edward Island. He and his crew reduced sail to a single reefed riding and foresail and let her run through the stormy night. Sometime during the storm *Vera B* missed Cheticamp's harbour. That night the crew dropped anchor to try to ride out the wind until morning when their exact position could be determined.

In the night the wind shifted forcing Captain Gillard to change tactics. Anchor chains were slipped to let her drive ashore, hopefully on a beach. But the little schooner grounded far from shore. With tremendous seas sweeping her decks all the four men could do was climb the rigging. For six hours they waited for the seas to abate. A life-saving station could be seen some distance away but, due to breakers rolling on the shore, little help could come from there. Gillard said, "I don't see any chance for saving our lives unless we loose the spars and try to get ashore on the wreckage."

Hedley Snook saw a solution. "Captain," he said, "if you lash me to a lifebuoy, I'll try to get to land." Gillard was doubtful, but finally agreed. Snook, young and strong at 22, reassured them, "It's just as well to take the risk than to stay here and perish in the rigging."

With those words, after waiting for three big waves to pass by, Snook bade goodbye to his shipmates, jumped over the side into the raging sea and made for shore. Snook was driven under water, rolled, tossed and beaten to shore on the breakers tumbling under the rocks, but finally made land more dead than alive. When he regained consciousness, he found himself in bed in the home of a French-speaking family named Ludley.

By some superhuman effort Snook dragged himself to the rescuers on the beach and made them understand he wanted a stronger rope attached to the line he had brought ashore. The heavy rope was attached to a dory which Gillard, Mosher and Warren pulled to *Vera B*. Only one man could come at a time: Warren first, then Mosher and Gillard pulled the dory back to the wreck. It was hours before all were safe on shore where residents cared for them. Exposed to the elements, *Vera B* eventually went to pieces.

None received the battering that Hedley Snook endured. After a few days the last three men off the wreck went home, but Snook remained in a Halifax hospital throughout the winter of 1923-24. While there he had sand and kelp pumped from his stomach. In April he returned to Fortune where the local doctor treated him for some time. After three months in other hospitals, Snook was finally pronounced fit and able to continue his sea-going life — almost a year from the time of his heoric deeds. However, Hedley Snook never fully recovered from his ordeal and he received no medals or recognition for his selfless bravery, but only the satisfaction of doing what he could in a seemingly hopeless situation.

Chapter 8 (1924)
"Rum row" and weather:
a tragic combination

Not many ships stranded on rocky shores escape unscathed. In rare instances off-loading cargo and the rising tide lifted a vessel from the death grip of an offshore ledge. Rare were the schooners pulled from beaches or jagged reefs by tugs. Once a ship grounds near shore the force of the breaking waves and the impact against unyielding rocks will smash boats or rafts to pieces. Any attempts at self-rescue are usually thwarted by pounding surf and rocks.

The force of a breaking wave — upwards of 2,000 pounds a square foot — snaps stanchions and thick planks, wrenches off steel plates and washes away deckhouses. So often the fall and winter gales make short work of victims trapped on an unforgiving shore.

North Shore steamer ashore at Long Point

Newspapers of August 1924 shouted, "Violent Tropical Storm: Wrecks Strew Nova Scotia Coastline" and when the storm abated officials tallied the shipping losses.

The August Gale of 1924 — localized to the Cape Breton coast — pounced on unsuspecting ships on August 24-25. On the evening of August 23, the 32-ton *Magno* with Captain Levi Baggs left Sydney for Port aux Basques, but he and his four crewmen never reported and probably went down in the storm.

The disappearance of Newfoundland-owned *Magno* proved to be one of the worst disasters of the storm. Another vessel, *Julia F.C.*, was first reported missing but was spotted near the entrance to St. Ann's Bay, crippled and dragging her anchors. *Julia F.C.* with her crew of Captain Devon of Sydney, Fred and William Anderson of North Sydney, and W. Gunderson, left North Sydney on August 26. She survived the storm but had her jib torn away and the mainmast broken off at the hounds, where the crosstrees join the mast.

According to Captain Anderson of the fishing vessel *Katrina II*, he had sailed near enough to *Julia F.C.* to discover her cabin was badly smashed, but the schooner had a dory trailing behind. On account of the rough seas, Anderson could not get close to the stricken vessel, but sounded his horn nine times. No one came on deck, thus on reaching North Sydney he immediately reported her whereabouts and condition to officials.

Aspy lies a derelict with windows boarded up. (Photo courtesy of North Sydney Museum)

Aspy, a well-known passenger steamer, was also caught out in the 50-mile-an-hour gale and shroud of rain. She nosed her way along the North Shore of Cape Breton on a regular trip from Bay St. Lawrence, near Cape North, to Sydney.

Built in Shelburne in 1910 for the passenger trade, the 99-ton *Aspy* regularly plied the route from Bay St. Lawrence to Sydney. In fair weather the little steamer usually left Bay St. Lawrence on a Tuesday evening, sailing to White Point, Neil's Harbour or Ingonish depending on tide and wind conditions, and on Wednesday morning began the last leg of her journey to Sydney calling at various ports along the way. Nine of her crew in August 1927 were Captain Yorke, mate Albert Nicholson, cook Vincent Welsh, Patrick Strumps, Patrick Ryan, Thomas Janes, Fred Martell, Walter LaFriend of North Ingonish, and George Buchanan of River Bennett.

On August 26 she had begun her trip to Sydney stopping first in White Point. When the wind came up overnight, the captain received a message from the North Shore Steamship Company, who managed the steamer, that *Aspy* had to be moved to a safer anchorage probably in Sydney. Captain Yorke tried and navigated in high winds and seas along the coastline near Cape Egmont, described as having "a dangerous reef which stretches about a mile out into the sea from the mainland and at high water is entirely submerged."

The captain kept nosing her out, but the gale-force wind pushed *Aspy* nearer the shoals about eight miles southeast of Aspy Bay. At the time *Aspy* carried freight and sixty passengers. In the informative book *Down North*, edited by Ron Caplan (1980), Walter LaFriend described the moment she struck: "I heard a thump. I knew she had to be striking bottom because she started rolling . . . She was ashore in an awful place. We couldn't see anything where we were. But we were lucky she went where she did — between Long Point and French Cove, near Neil's Harbour. If she went up a little farther and struck on what we call Long Point, there'd be nobody got ashore. Impossible, because it's all breakers there. I opened the galley door and there was the sea coming right aboard of her. We went to see the captain to get the lifeboats out."

At first Yorke felt it might be possible to back her off, but the engineer reported the main steam pipe had broken off. *Aspy* was impaled on a rock embedded through the cargo hold.

One of the crew struggled to get a lifeboat to shore, made a rope secure and with the aid of some men on land and the rest on the wrecked steamer, pulled the lifeboat back and forth until all passengers were safely ashore. Within a few days the well-known passenger ship *Aspy* was reduced to debris. Crewman George Buchanan in *Down North* commented on her wreck: "It took an awful storm to break her up — she was well built. Big timbers in her, but that was a stormy night."

Other vessels wrecked in the storm were *Lady Thorburn*, a 62-ton ship out of St. John's, stranded to total loss near L'Ardoise, and the tern schooner *Anna MacDonald* at Kitty Witty Shoals near Prospect.

Unsolved mystery at Prospect

The circumstances under which the 112-foot long schooner *Anna MacDonald* went to her doom on Kitty Witty Shoals off Prospect will likely never be known. Sometime during the August Gale of 1924, the schooner was lost and her five crew members, including Captain Miller, became victims of the sea. The 192-ton *Anna MacDonald* was built in Cardigan, Prince Edward Island, in 1920 and was registered there.

Boats from Prospect visited the wreck on the east side of Kitty Witty Shoals, but could find no indication of what had become of the crew; there were no bodies aboard and no personal effects. Captain Miller — who at age 55 left a wife, a son and two daughters, one of whom resided at Stanley Bridge, PEI — knew the coastline as did two of his crewmen, Claude Archibald and Edward Purcell of Prospect. Purcell had sailed on *Anna MacDonald* for a year. Two other crewmen, Joseph Rogers and Henry Brown, belonged to New Brunswick.

For seamen not familiar with the area, the entrance to Prospect can be hazardous as it is narrow, flanked by shoals and small islands. In early September the ship's boat was located, battered to pieces.

Reports of damage to shipping showed the storm had cut a wide swath. At Yarmouth Bar, *Lizzie E* was wrecked. Joseph Watkins of Yarmouth Bar lost his life, while his brother and the rest of the crew escaped. Watkins was survived by his wife and two children. At sea the transoceanic liner *Arabic* was mauled by the August Gale winds, estimated by the captain to be in excess of 100 miles an hour. More than fifty passengers were injured; lifeboats were swept over the side and several port-hole windows smashed.

Other news coming out of the August Gale of 1924 would be more devastating.

Tragedy out of Mahone Bay, Lunenburg, LaHave

Reports by the fishing fleet returning from George's Bank in late September 1924 were not good. Two American schooners, *Ingomar* and *Natalie Hammond*, located a capsized schooner near George's Bank. Although a lookout was posted to search for a dory or her crew, no sign of them was ever found. News came back to the *Sydney Post* which headlined on September 30, 1924, "Tern Schooner Capsizes with all Hands, Tragedy of Rum Row is Unfolded."

Beryl M. Corkum was a victim of a death-dealing hurricane which swept the North Atlantic the third week of August, 1924. But her fate was wrapped up in another phenomenon of the time. She had cleared from Halifax in June with a cargo of liquor for the United States coast and was supposed to have left "Rum Row" before the August 26 hurricane.

In 1919 the United States adopted the National Prohibition Act making the production, sale and distribution of liquor illegal. Enforcement of the law through the Volstead Act spawned a new and turbulent era on North America's east coast as people continued to purchase hard-to-get alcohol — a period of lawbreaking that lasted fourteen years until Prohibition was repealed in December 1933.

The French islands of St. Pierre and Miquelon, a few miles off Newfoundland's South Coast, took on a major distribution role supplying rum, whisky and wine to Newfoundland, Canadian and American smugglers. Often Nova Scotian and Newfoundland schooners took the products from St. Pierre or the West Indies to the twelve mile limit off the eastern seaboard of the United States, commonly referred to as Rum Row. There they were met by American liquor buyers, who illegally transported the goods into New York, New Jersey and other states.

Schooners took chances with wind and weather to avoid detection, to deliver "the goods" on time, or to return for another load. Such was the case of the tern schooner *Beryl M. Corkum*. She had been heard from as sailing "from sea" in ballast on August 22, one day prior to the notorious August Gale of 1924. Her destination was Lunenburg, but *Corkum* had not reported.

She had long been known along the coast as one of the vessels plying from Bridgetown, Barbados, to Halifax and to St. Pierre — a deadly triangle in the rum traffic trade with one stop on the route, the American coast. *Beryl M. Corkum* had cleared from Halifax on May 25, 1924, with 4,000 cases of liquor under charter to American interests. The cargo had been dropped off and she set sail in ballast for Nova Scotia. Her ship's stores, food and equipment were supplied by Lunenburg Outfitting Company, but the vessel was not insured.

The American fishing crews who reported the wreck said she was floating bottom up, in a manner that clearly showed her name and hailing port but prevented any examination of the cabins, decks, masts or topsides of the vessel.

Beryl M. Corkum originally sailed from Lunenburg, but her registry had been changed to Bridgetown, Barbados, several months before. She netted 248 tons and had been built in LaHave in 1914. Her lost crew were: Captain William Zwicker, who left a wife and two children; the captain's son-in-law Arthur Zwicker, also survived by his wife and two children; Charles Wynacht, survived by his wife and six children; Titus Westhaver — all from Mahone Bay; Charles Ernst from Lunenburg who was single; mate Gabriel Corkum, who left a wife in LaHave; and Alphonzo Branes from Barbados.

Rum-running was a lucrative trade but, as the US Coast Guard increased in strength and in surveillance techniques, it became dangerous and virtually impossible to continue smuggling. High speed chases and gunfire became more common. Sea pursuits climaxed when the Coast Guard fired on and sank a Canadian vessel and well-known rum-runner — *I'm Alone* — 200 miles from the United States, drowning one of the crew and risking the lives of others.

Before that dispute was completed, another controversy arose. In September 1929 another incident pushed the conflict between Canadian rum-runners and the American Coast Guard onto the front pages. On September 11 the Nova Scotian motor vessel *Shawnee* was shelled by the

USCG ship *Number 145* while *Shawnee* was off Ambrose Light near New York harbour. Her crew was L. Lohnes, V. Mosher and C. Young of Lunenburg, A. Comeau, L. Silverman, L. Rormain of Meteghan, and Cecil Bayers of Halifax.

According to the American version of the pursuit, *Shawnee* was running without lights and her name and hailing port to identify her was not on the stern. Captain McLeod of *Shawnee* denied this, saying when she was launched the previous year at Meteghan the name was painted on the stern. McLeod described the pursuit at sea: "When the *No. 145* sighted us, she turned in pursuit. We were running and showing all lights and with the Canadian ensign on the mainmast. *No. 145* came within ten yards and fired three shots. Remaining close on our port side the Coast Guard vessel then turned on her searchlight and hailed me asking, 'What ship is that?' To which I replied, 'Well you should know,' or words to that effect."

On January 25, 1931, William Cluett of Belleoram, Newfoundland, was shot and killed by gunfire from a US Coast Guard vessel. Cluett had been engaged in illegal activities on the rum-runner *Josephine K.*

When Franklin D. Roosevelt became president of the United States in 1932, he realized Prohibition had failed to abolish bootlegging, rum-running and the widespread lawbreaking associated with it. He put in place the Twenty-first Amendment which on December 5, 1933, repealed Prohibition. The dramatic era of troubles and sea pursuits between two otherwise friendly neighbours, Canada and the United States, officially ended.

South Ingonish: end of *Douglas H. Thomas*

Douglas H. Thomas, a dependable workhorse in and around Sydney harbour and once demolished in the Halifax Explosion, found her final rest at South Ingonish.

After the 1917 Explosion the tugboat had been refitted and rebuilt from "stem to stern." Originally built in Maryland, USA, in 1892 the steel, 116-foot-long *D. H. Thomas*, or *Thomas* as she was sometimes called, came to Nova Scotia in 1899. During her stay she had been at the scene of many a wreck; some of the more notable were the S.S. *Bruce*, 1911, *Annie Roberts*, 1913, *Harold C. Beecher* and *Cienfuegos*, 1914, and the loss of *Volunda* in 1921.

Surviving the brunt of the Halifax Explosion was not her only tribulation. On November 13, 1912, in Sydney harbour the steamer *City of Sydney* and *Douglas H. Thomas* collided. *City of Sydney* had been docked at Ingraham's Wharf all that day and, when she was ready to sail about 9:30 p.m., engaged the tug to tow her out. *Douglas H. Thomas'* crew attached the hawsers and both vessels headed down the harbour abreast. At ten p.m. the larger steamer struck the tug a glancing blow about midships. *Douglas H. Thomas* keeled over and began to fill with water. The captain turned *Thomas* around and headed for shore at full speed to save her from going to the bottom.

Douglas H. Thomas had on board thirty-eight stevedores, who had been working on *City of Sydney* all day and were being taken back to North Sydney and home. Five men on *Thomas* could not be accounted for and presumably had been knocked overboard on impact: stevedores Fred Sams, about 26 years old, J. Sams, C. Pike, Charles Evans, and John Grover, a deckhand also about 26. All five hailed from Newfoundland.

As small boats went out grappling the bottom for bodies, Harbour Traffic Manager MacIsaac ordered *City of Sydney* to stand by until the accident was investigated. By November 16, three bodies had been recovered: Grover, Evans, and Fred Sams. *Douglas H. Thomas* was pumped out, pulled off the beach and examined, but she had received little damage. A subsequent official inquiry found both captains at fault.

Douglas H. Thomas' career continued for another twelve years until October 4, 1924, when she was wrecked at South Ingonish. At Ingonish *Thomas* would take scows in tow for the dredging of Louisbourg harbour. She had already safely delivered Public Works Dredge Number 11 to Louisbourg.

Captain Lay cautiously felt his way into Ingonish knowing the channel, about 180 feet wide, to be dangerous and the only one available for boats drawing any amount of water. Most of her crew were on deck when she hit and, with her bottom smashed, they soon felt her settle in the water. The crew — Captain Lay, first mate P. Campbell, chief engineer J. O'Rourke, second engineer David Jackson, steward or cook L. McIntyre, sailors Frank Vaulice and T. Lay, firemen J.A. McKinnon, A. Edwards, and M. Lay — left at once in lifeboats leaving their belongings behind.

Ten minutes after she hit, *Douglas H. Thomas* was practically submerged with only her stern peeking above water. With the spate of fine weather and calm seas, it was first thought she could be refloated but it was not to be. The tug *Lingan*, which brought some of the crew back to Sydney, returned to the site of the wreck with coal company officials and George Robertson, the company diver. With her bottom torn out, the cost of repair exceeded the vessel's worth.

Dominion Coal decried her loss saying she was a first class ship in every respect, powerful dependable and good looking.

Passenger steamer burns in Bras d'Or Lake

"Abandon ship!" Captain MacDonald shouted the order. As the S.S. *Bras d'Or's* lifeboat was being launched, the wheelhouse and cabin, which had been burning madly, caved in. It was about 6:15 a.m. December 11, 1924. The crew and passengers rowed for shore watching the vessel sink.

Bras d'Or was on her regular passenger run when about five miles off Cape Around, Bras d'Or Lake in Richmond County, someone saw smoke coming from below deck. Captain MacDonald ordered the hose lines connected immediately and in three minutes the crew had a powerful jet of water directed on the flames. MacDonald shut the engines down since the forward motion of the steamer fanned the flames, now licking at the deck.

After a vigorous battle with the fire for fifteen to twenty minutes, it was clear to all the ship was doomed. Under great difficulty amid dense clouds of smoke and steam the men lowered the lifeboat. By this time the fire had made such headway it was impossible to stand on deck. Six passengers — four adults and two children — the crew and captain climbed into the lifeboat at the very moment the wheelhouse and cabin collapsed in flames.

In thirty minutes the 136-ton *Bras d'Or* had burned to the water's edge and was completely destroyed. According to the captain, the cause of the fire was not clear but judging from where the flames had broken through it had started behind the steam boiler.

S.S. *Bras d'Or*, built in Mahone Bay around five years before at a cost of $125,000, was one of the finest steamers of her class on the Atlantic coast. It was the second shipping loss for her owners in less than a year: *Aspy* had wrecked at White Point in the August Gale four months earlier.

A narrow passage: Main-à-Dieu and Scaterie

The year 1924 had almost drawn to a close when a ship crashed ashore in the narrow waterway between Scaterie Island and the mainland.

On Wednesday December 25, S.S. *Curlew*, with Captain Dominic LeBlanc at the helm, left Sydney for Canso with a cargo of coal. By 4:30 p.m. Friday, *Curlew* began her return trip to Sydney. At midnight the steamer was negotiating the worst part of the Main-à-Dieu Passage — a channel of about a half mile of "good water" bordered by shoals and sunken rocks. At the most critical moment, part of the steering gear gave out allowing the steamer to swing off her course and head directly for the rocks. Captain LeBlanc immediately ordered the engines reversed in an attempt to back clear of the shoal and for a while it looked possible.

The engine room crew had already set to work to repair the broken steering apparatus and had been busy for some time when it was discovered *Curlew* was taking on water rapidly. Several feet of water was found in the hold — evidence that some plates had worked loose, although none of the crew had felt the vessel strike the rocks. The captain had no explanation. It was thought the impact came just as the engines were reversed. The noise and shuddering of *Curlew* on the sudden change from full speed ahead to full astern acted as a counter to the shock of striking the reef. Now that she was unmanageable and helpless in the strong current, the fight for her life was short. She went to the bottom a little after daylight Saturday morning, December 27, 1924. The crew landed in Main-à-Dieu and from there went to Sydney.

Owned in Sydney, the 100-foot-long *Curlew* was twenty-nine years old, built for government service, and patterned after naval craft of her day with a ram bow and a hull of steel. Her top gallant sail and high forecastle made her conspicuous in every port. She had been purchased by W.N. McDonald in 1918. Valued at $30,000 she was insured for two-thirds of that amount.

"Tern Schooners on LaHave River" 1930

Daniel Getson (above) was a 295-net-ton tern schooner built at Bridgewater in 1917. She had a long life around Nova Scotia's shores, but was eventually sold to someone in the US in 1958 and renamed *Wanderthirst*. Like many local ships sold to foreign owners, her end is obscure. (Postcard photo courtesy of Jack Keeping)

Chapter 9 (1925-30)
The winds of autumn

Ashore at Canso

The new year 1925 was only a few weeks old when the first shipping casualty happened. *Margaretville* of the Canso branch of the Maritime Fish Cooperative went ashore on January 24, 1925, in the Strait of Canso and was lost. A northwest gale which sprang up without warning pushed *Margaretville* onto the rocks. Her crew was taken off by the freight steamer *Robert G. Cann* and landed at Mulgrave.

Foundered off D'Escousse

Each winter was bound to bring some casualties to the Nova Scotian schooner fleet and 1925 was no exception. On January 25 *Acadian*, whose managing owner was W.P. Bartlett of North Sydney, was pierced by ice and sunk off D'Escousse. Captain Lake and his crew of six barely had time to escape with what clothes they wore.

This was a vessel plagued by bad luck. Three months previously she had left St. Pierre and was blown off course by one of the worst storms of the year. Eventually she reached Souris, PEI, where she loaded a full cargo of produce for Mr. Acorn of Souris. En route to St. Pierre, *Acadian* became frozen in the ice. S.S. *Montcalm* came to her assistance and freed her, but it was one delay after another until *Acadian* went to her doom off D'Escousse.

Collision on the Banks

The fishing season of 1925 brought sadness to many families when the Cunard ocean liner *Tuscania* rammed the halibut schooner *Rex*. In the dense fog southeast of Quero Bank, Captain Thomas O. Downie and thirteen crewmen of *Rex*, as well as the 10-year-old son of the cook, met their deaths on Sunday, June 29, as the schooner was lying to east of Sable Island.

Although manned mostly by Nova Scotians, the 75-ton *Rex* was American owned and had been built in Essex, Massachusetts, in 1908. She carried a crew of twenty-four. Nine men were on deck, but the rest, including the boy who was asleep in his father's bunk while enjoying a school vacation on the high seas, were below relaxing, lying down or talking. Those on deck kept a sharp watch, blowing the horn at frequent intervals but no sounds of a steamer's whistle could be heard.

Suddenly out of the fog came the liner *Tuscania*. Due to the fog and heavy weather, she was off her regular course. She cut into *Rex* on the port bow and sliced through the schooner, her bow coming out of the starboard side just forward of the main rigging. The foremast was ripped out and smashed. Forty tons of ice in *Rex*'s holds fell into the sea around the wreckage. What remained of *Rex* went under water in the impact, resurfacing as debris.

The men on the starboard side were flung into the water among the debris and floating ice. They had no time to shout a warning to those below and if they had had the time to warn them, it was not likely the men below could have escaped, so quickly did *Tuscania* bear down. The cook was seen running down into the forecastle to save his son, but neither was ever seen again.

Following the collision, *Tuscania* slowly came to a stop then lowered her lifeboats. The schooner was no longer in sight. Bits of wood, broken dories and deck gear littered the surrounding ocean. Nine survivors —

engineer Albert Roberts, Ralph Clayton, Edward Surrette, James O'Brien, Thomas Flannigan, Daniel Grady, Edgar Muise, Edward Fralick, and Alfred Hubbard — were located as well as the captain's body. Those lost on *Rex* were Captain Thomas A. Downie of Jordan River, George Johnson, Joseph Dalton, Angus Smith, Angus D. McDonald, Clyde Larkin, Samuel Tibbits, Charles Goodick, William Roach, William Turner, Archie Hill, Oscar Williams, Charles Weiball, the cook Austin Firth and his son Charles Austin both of Jordan Branch.

Inez G — double tragedy near Lingan Head

Caught in a violent September gale, Captain Joseph Vatcher and his crew valiantly tried to reach North Sydney. Three miles from port, while off Lingan, *Inez G* was pushed over on her side. She was completely engulfed in water three or four times and then sank.

Captain Vatcher of Burgeo fought the gale to the end and was heard by one of the two survivors saying, "If she goes down, I'll go down with her." Both survivors — Kenneth Bragg of Burgeo and George Bungay who resided in North Sydney — told how captain and crew had remained at their posts all day and battled the storm.

Built in 1911 and classed as a semi-knockabout, the 66-ton *Inez G*, once owned on the northeast coast of Newfoundland and commanded by Captain George Gulliford, was sold to Burgeo men. According to the *Sydney Post* of January 15, 1925, *Inez G* left North Sydney for Barbados on what was believed to be the earliest voyage south of any vessel that year. For several days she had been at the wharf loading empty kegs. At Barbados she was due to go into dry dock and then sail for Demerara, home of the sparkling and much sought after rum. Upon her return to American and Nova Scotian waters she lay off the Cape Breton coast disposing of her cargo. Much of it had been unloaded when the September gale hit the Nova Scotia coast without warning.

All through Friday September 25, 1925, the Burgeo schooner withstood a battering from nature's worst elements, but that night Vatcher discovered she had begun to leak from the severe pounding. *Inez G* was riding out the storm at anchor with her two anchors holding firm, but water rising in the holds forced a run to North Sydney. Around nine p.m. a heavy squall turned her over on her side.

While at anchor off Nova Scotia, George Bungay and Wheeler, two men employed as swordfishermen on another boat, had transferred to *Inez G* to get a passage to North Sydney from the fishing grounds. On the night *Inez G* sank she fell over on her side. Bungay tore a dory loose from its lashings and jumped into it. Bragg was swept off the tilting deck by a heavy sea and was carried for some distance underwater by the sinking schooner. When he came to the surface he found himself by the side of the dory which had Bungay aboard. Bragg, weighted down with oilskins and wet clothes, grabbed the gunwales and with a superhuman effort Bungay pulled him in over the side.

They saw none of their comrades after the vessel fell over on her beam ends, although Bragg claimed to have heard someone shout frantically, "Oh my God! Oh my God!" Apart from that they neither heard nor saw any sign from their comrades. Both men fought their way through high seas and wind and after an arduous struggle against the elements reached the shore at Lingan. Exhausted and suffering from hypothermia, they were taken into Menzies Forward's house and cared for.

Captain Vatcher, who had intended to leave *Inez G* at the end of her trip and retire from the sea, formerly commanded the little Burgeo steamer *Herbert Green*. He had also owned the schooner *Julia F.C.* Six men — five from Burgeo, one from North Sydney — were lost and two survived.

Inez G's crew hailed from Burgeo: Vatcher; Edward Harris; John Hiscock, originally from Codroy but living in Burgeo; Robert Strickland, and another Robert Strickland (probably father and son). A sixth man James Wheeler, a passenger from North Sydney, was married with eight children. Vatcher left a wife and no children; both Stricklands were married with children. Harris and Hiscock were single.

CAPTAIN AND FOUR SEAMAN FIND A WATERY GRAVE THREE MILES FROM PORT

A Terrific Gale Struck the Schooner Inez G. Off the Cape Breton Coast, Turned Her Over on Her Side.—Sank in a Very Short Time, Carrying Six Men Down With Her.—Two Miraculously Saved.—Vessel Hailed From Burgeo, Newfoundland.

SYDNEY, N. S., September 26.—Captain Joseph Vatcher, of the 55-ton schooner Inez G., of Burgeo, Nfld., and five seamen were

The Halifax *Evening Mail* of September 26, 1925, headlined the loss of the Burgeo, Newfoundland, schooner *Inez G*.

A small unidentified schooner lies at anchor. The Burgeo schooner *Inez G* would have been about this size, much too small to be caught battling a vicious autumn gale. (Photo from the author's collection)

But the sea was not finished with *Inez G*. About a month later the derelict and much of its cargo of liquor drifted in near shore between Bridgeport/Westmount and Dominion. It eventually grounded on a reef three-quarters of a mile offshore and broke apart. Almost universally when wreckage comes near shore salvors attempt to secure whatever cargo or supplies they can. People near Lingan Head had already salvaged fifty barrels of rum and then, in early November, a new rumour added frenzied interest in the wreck of *Inez G*. It was said that Captain Vatcher had $7,000 stored in a chest aboard the ill-fated schooner. For hundreds of people lining the shore, pieces of the wreck, like the deck of the schooner, meant nothing as they searched for more valuable goods.

Bernard MacIntyre, aged 42, of Bridgeport had gone down to the beach with several other men to get casks which had drifted ashore between Bridgeport and Dominion. Five casks had already been successfully landed that day. MacIntyre spotted a cask a short distance from shore and took off his shoes to wade out. When near the flotsam, he apparently stepped into deeper water but continued swimming, got hold of the cask and tried to get it to land. He gave a cry for help and immediately sank before any others working a short distance away on the shore could help. MacIntyre, a miner by occupation, resided on MacIntyre's Lane, Bridgeport. He, his six brothers and a sister were well known in the area. His brother Peter, a Glace Bay town councillor, and Michael were on the Glace Bay police force.

Coast strewn with wrecks —
A.F. Davidson, South Head, Corean

The year 1926 was nearly over when a raging northeaster accompanied with heavy snow ravaged the eastern coast of Nova Scotia. The toll of ships rose to six schooners and three small steamers in the wake of the December 5-6 gale. Although no loss of life had been reported, the majority of the disasters came to craft torn from winter moorings and dashed on the shore.

The blizzard with winds up to seventy miles an hour lasted twenty-four hours. The largest vessel washed ashore was the four-masted *A.F. Davidson* on White Head, Grand Manan Island, New Brunswick — her crew saved by island coast guards. A tern schooner, *South Head*, in ballast from St. Pierre became a total loss at the entrance to Herring Cove. *William C. Smith*, a 99-ton schooner registered at Lunenburg and lumber-laden for New York, wrecked at Little Port Herbert. *Corean*, also loaded with lumber for New York, was a total loss at Quoddy. The fishing schooner *R.L. MacKenzie* was reported in difficulty at Lockeport. *Atlanta*, an 86-ton ship laden with potatoes, stranded at Low Point, Sydney. An unidentified ship beached near Lunenburg and a smaller vessel, the 17-ton *Ozma* owned in Lunenburg, broke adrift and stranded on Fox Island in Lunenburg Bay.

Alsatian, out of Lunenburg

The banking schooner *Alsatian* had been built in Chester, Nova Scotia, in 1923. Her measurements and form (116 feet long and 26.8 feet wide) were similar to that of the *Bluenose*, the renown racing schooner of Nova Scotia.

Like *Bluenose*, the *Alsatian* had fished out of Lunenburg in her time as a banker. Her first owner was the Alsatian Fishing Company of Lunenburg, a consortium of businessmen including E.F. Zwicker, Freeman Walters, and several fishing captains, including Angus Walters the captain of *Bluenose*. Many ship owners and builders in Lunenburg were of German descent and accordingly the schooner may have been christened *Alsatian*, a derivative of the word Alsace, a province of northern France near the German border. The 120-ton schooner began her career as a salt banker in the fall of 1923.

During the first week in April 1927, *Alsatian* fished the Western Bank securing 550 quintals (about 61,600 pounds) of cod — the good start indicated another successful fishing voyage. But on April 13, a typical spring storm forced the schooner to stop fishing and ride out a stiff northerly gale and a heavy sea.

Without warning, a huge wave broke over the *Alsatian* nearly sending her to Davey Jones' locker. Only the fact that she was battened down kept her holds from filling with water. Fortunately, none of the men working on deck were swept overboard. Captain Corkum, in command that year, later described the wall of water as "a small tidal wave." According to him, the wave was at least twenty feet high, reaching fifteen feet up the jumbo stay and completely engulfing the schooner. By the time the wave passed, Captain Corkum had crashed against the windlass and suffered broken ribs; Robert Corkum of Nova Scotia (no relation to the captain) was dying from head and body injuries; Albert Janes of Rencontre, Newfoundland, was taken from beneath the debris of three dories with his leg broken; and Samuel Brown of Burin suffered a wrenched shoulder.

Seven dories were reduced to kindling and others were torn from their lashings and scattered over the deck. The deck engine and chain locker were smashed. Furthermore, the impact of tons of water jarred the vessel's timbers and she was leaking. Forced to abandon fishing, *Alsatian* returned to Lunenburg with her flag at half-mast — symbolizing another death at sea — for the injured fisherman passed away on his vessel before she reached port.

Far greater tragedy befell the sailing schooner after she was brought to Grand Bank, Newfoundland, by Samuel H. Patten. In May 1933, Patten had lost the banker *Dorothy Melita* when she struck an iceberg and sank on the Grand Banks. Purchased to replace her, the *Alsatian* was brought to Grand Bank that summer.

On the morning of March 3, 1935, the *Alsatian* left Harbour Breton. With Captain Jim Lawrence was a cook, a deck boy, and a crew of twenty-two Fortune Bay fishermen to man her eleven dories. Later in the evening as *Alsatian*, *Pauline Lohnes*, *Robert Esdale* and other South Coast bankers left Fortune Bay, the wind picked up to a strong easterly, veering at night to a bitterly cold, gale-force northwesterly, the worst of winter winds.

Other vessels sought shelter in St. Pierre until the vicious storm abated, but the *Alsatian*'s captain chose not to stop and sailed on into a dark, cold March night and oblivion, never to be seen nor heard of again. No floating wreckage was ever found. The relentless ocean had silently and completely claimed the Nova Scotian-built schooner and her Newfoundland crew.

Lunenburg vessels, victims of the August Gale

In September 1927, as the Nova Scotia banking fleet was due to return, several Lunenburg schooners failed to report: *Una R. Corkum*, Captain Wilfred Andrews; *Mahala*, Captain Warren Knickle; *Clayton Walters*, Captain Mars Selig; and *Joyce C. Smith*, with Captain Edward Maxner and nineteen Newfoundland fishermen. The story of the four Lunenburg schooners has been recounted in other books and their fate, although significant and tragic, will not be retold here. But a fifth vessel *Columbia*, also lost in the August Gale, had a Nova Scotian connection.

Columbia, of Gloucester, Massachusetts, one of the few schooners to ever come close to taking the Fisherman's Trophy away from the great Canadian racer *Bluenose*, disappeared that terrible August gale. On September 12, 1927, five of her dories were found on Sable Island. Months later, another wrecked dory confirmed the loss of the *Columbia*, Captain Warton, and his twenty-two men. Three of the twenty-two resided in Halifax: Joseph Mayo, his eldest son Albert, and his youngest son, George Henry.

Riverport schooner total loss

On the last day of September 1927, *Manuata* grounded in dense fog at the entrance of the LaHave River. She was leaving Riverport under charter to travel to Burin, Newfoundland, to load fish destined for Marseilles, France.

Built in Liverpool in 1919, the 114-ton *Manuata* had been employed for years as a fishing vessel skippered by Frank Risser. Due a scarcity of fishermen she stayed in Riverport all summer, then arrangements were made for a new crew to take her across to France. The crew was Captain Harry Ritcey, mate Angus Romkey, cook Vernon Wilkie, and seamen George Hickman, Urban Covey, Alex Green, and another unidentified sailor.

Manuata ran into dense fog off the mouth of the LaHave River causing the vessel to deviate from her course. Before Captain Ritcey could swing her clear of the rocks he saw ahead, she grounded on the west side of Gass Island. Word spread of *Manuata*'s predicament and by the evening of October 1, two steamers (*Arras* and *Mascot)* and the tug *O.K. Service* were standing by. The crew left *Manuata* without incident but rough seas made it impossible to attempt to refloat the schooner. When the wind came up *Manuata*, by now taking on water, pounded heavily on the shore. Although she was later towed off, she was declared a total loss.

Stranded on Scaterie

When *Admiral Drake* was lost on Scaterie Island, located on the eastern tip of Cape Breton, it became a matter of how and when the crew would get off the island.

On November 26, 1927, the tern schooner grounded on the shores of Scaterie. At 8:30 p.m. while en route to Sydney from St. John's she struck Eastern Rock, filled with water and broke apart. Captain Arnold Benson, mate Leonard Dale, bosun Armand Segullian, cook William Pike, and seamen Michael Lenham, Albert Parsons, William Kerrivan, and Raymond Murray, all of St. John's, reached shore in their own boats. For four days wind and heavy seas prevented the castaways from reaching the mainland. When weather abated they travelled to Sydney and from there made their way to Newfoundland.

Built in Shelburne in 1916 *Admiral Drake*, netting 309 tons, was the largest tern schooner launched by builder G.A. Cox up to that year. She measured 130 feet long and 32 feet wide. Owner A.S. Rendell and Company of St. John's had her in general trade. At the time of her loss, she carried no cargo but ballast.

The *Daily News* of November 29, 1927, described the plight of *Admiral Drake*'s crew stranded on Scaterie.

Four or five days later, the Italian steamer *Generale Demitti* sighted part of *Drake*'s hull off Flint Island, about three miles from Scaterie. On December 1, the captain of S.S. *Haugerland* informed Vincent Mullins of the Marine and Fisheries Department at Sydney that the wrecked schooner had split from end to end and floated in two sections off Flint Island. The government cutter *Margaret* was sent to remove the wreckage, a menace to navigation.

Mayotte out of Lunenburg

On February 1, 1928, when she was about halfway between Halifax and Bermuda, the Lunenburg schooner *Mayotte*, commanded by Captain Joseph Himmelman, became a drifting derelict. In the off-season from fishing *Mayotte*, one of the prolific fleet that made Lunenburg a name upon the seas, delivered dried fish to the West Indies.

Meagre dispatches coming back to Nova Scotia described how she drifted abandoned "with her flag flying" — a poignant tribute to the loss of life that accompanied her loss. Another vessel and one more life was added to the long list of Lunenburg schooners and sailors lost at sea during 1927-28.

Several hours before the rescue of *Mayotte*'s company, Albert Zinck, a member of the crew, was swept from her deck in the height of the storm. The remaining men were in imminent danger of death, until they were rescued by Captain Manning and the Canadian government merchant marine ship *Canadian Pathfinder*, outbound from Halifax for Bermuda and the British West Indies with passengers and freight.

Mayotte sailed from Lunenburg on January 27 for Ponce, Puerto Rico, with a cargo of 500 tierces, or large casks, of dry cod and 150 tierces of salt herring. She had covered about half the distance between Lunenburg and Bermuda when disaster came upon her. Buffeted by a storm that had stripped her of sails and swept her decks clear of dories and gear, *Mayotte*'s crew fought the seas for thirteen days. Albert Zinck was hurled to his death in the dark swirling waters on a Sunday night.

Rescue arrived at two o'clock Monday morning. Flares from the plunging *Mayotte* burst out of the dark storm and then disappeared, but it was sufficient to make known to *Pathfinder*'s watch that somewhere in the trough of the sea, men were struggling against a merciless adversary. In later reports, Manning did not give much detail of his part in the rescue, but by what he described of the condition of the schooner it was assumed that the men on the vessel were without dories, in which case *Pathfinder* in all probability sent out one of her boats to take the survivors off the derelict.

Mayotte was about 375 miles south of Halifax on the Halifax–Bermuda lane when she was abandoned at latitude 39.24 north, longitude 63.59 west. By then, she had eight feet of her hull above the water line and still had her flag flying. The surviving crew members, who were taken to Bermuda by *Pathfinder*, were Captain Joseph Himmelman, mate William DeCourcey, George Myra, Clarence Tancock, all of Lunenburg, cook Naaman Wentzell from Riverport, and Elleur Cuthran, a native of Sweden. Once the survivors were safely off the sinking schooner, Captain Manning of *Pathfinder* sent this message which was relayed to Zwicker and Company on Monday: "At two a.m. this morning, picked off Captain and five men from schooner *Mayotte*. Albert Zinck washed overboard last night. Will land crew at Bermuda."

For several days *Mayotte*, the prey of Atlantic storms, as an abandoned hulk was a danger to ships in the Canada–Bermuda sea lanes. So the commander of *Canadian Pathfinder* requested his head office at Montreal to notify the Department of Marine and Fisheries to issue warnings to all shipping in the area.

Built in Mahone Bay in 1924, *Mayotte* had an overall length of 126 feet, a 26-foot beam, an 11-foot depth of hold, and registered 99-tons. She was the highliner or top producer in the Lunenburg fishing fleet during 1927.

Maud Thornhill — In mid-January 1929, rum-runner *Maud Thornhill* was posted as missing. On February 2, M.V. *Firelight*, owned by the same LaHave interests as *Maud Thornhill*, stopped at Halifax to report she had been searching for the schooner. *Maud Thornhill*, built in 1915 at Shelburne, had sailed from Halifax for St. John's on January 3, 1929, but was so long overdue that Nova Scotian interests reported her crew — Captain Robert Mosher of Lower LaHave, cook Robert Walters of LaHave, engineer Alexander Dunphy of Cape Breton, and Herbert Kirby, Edwin Walsh, John Moulton and Walter Brown of Burin, Newfoundland — lost at sea. All turned up safely weeks later. Mosher later explained that he and his crew were delayed by high seas and weather. (Photo courtesy of US Coast Guard, Washington DC)

Seal Island Shoals claim a ship

The crack fishing schooner *Josephine de Costa*, out of Boston, struck a submerged rock off Seal Island on September 17, 1929. *De Costa*, as she was known, was one of the speediest and most successful schooners of the American fleet. She had left Boston the day previous bound for Brown's Bank off Nova Scotia to search for cod and haddock, but grounded near Seal Island tearing a large hole in her side. Under the direction of Captain Stillman, the crew of twenty-two tried unsuccessfully to save *Josephine de Costa*. They launched the dories and rowed into Pubnico.

Margaret K. Smith, built in 1922 at Lunenburg's Smith and Rhuland yards — the same business had constructed the champion racer *Bluenose* the previous year — competed in the schooner races against the best sailors of Nova Scotia. On September 21, 1929, under Captain Whynacth she won at Lunenburg's Fisheries Exhibition and Fishermen's Reunion by defeating *Leah Beryl* and Captain Lawrence Zinck, and *Shirley Corkum* under Captain Foster Corkum. In 1935 *Margaret K. Smith* had outlived her usefulness as a Nova Scotian banking schooner and was sold to Kearley Brothers at Belleoram, Newfoundland. She disappeared with her crew a few miles off Halifax in August 1943, the time and cause of her disappearance has never been determined. (Photo courtesy of Public Archives of Nova Scotia)

Bound down for Sheet Harbour:
marooned at Gilford Island

Hippolyta II had been laid up, unwanted and unused, at Brookfield's Wharf, Halifax, for a lengthy period. In the summer of 1929 Captain William Munroe of Mushaboom purchased the small motor vessel and made ready to travel to Sheet Harbour, the major port near his hometown. Travelling with him were his wife and Arthur Monroe, who resided in Halifax. Early Friday afternoon, September 13, *Hippolyta II* and her small crew steamed out of Halifax harbour. At nine o'clock Saturday night, off Taylor's Head and practically within sight of their destination, the engine failed.

Monroe let down the anchor, but with the wind increasing south-westerly *Hippolyta II* dragged her anchor and drifted to within 200 yards southwest of Gilford Island. There the anchor caught a firm hold again. The three desperate sailors needed every advantage but it was not to be. Having been laid up so long, equipment aboard the little craft was not in the best condition and the old hawser chaffed off. Pinned between pounding surf and the island cliffs, *Hippolyta II* was doomed. All three jumped off the deck.

Heavy seas washed Mrs. Monroe off the rocks and into the breaking combers. Her husband jumped into the sea to rescue her and was in danger of being dragged under himself when Arthur Monroe threw a rope to them. Both held the rope as Monroe pulled them in through the breakers. Mrs. Monroe was bruised and badly shaken up.

They soon realized they were on a small island with no way to get off. Six or seven hours later, they found enough debris and driftwood to fashion a crude distress signal flag which was seen by James V. Kenney, lightkeeper of Sheet Rock Light Station. By the time Kenney got them off the island and to the light station nearly twenty-four hours had passed since *Hippolyta II* had broken up. *Hippolyta II* was not covered by insurance and the Monroes lost all belongings they had carried with them.

On November 14, 1929, *The Halifax Herald* reported the small steamer *Judique* had sunk off Scaterie three days previously. The crew — Captain Garland Crewe, William Anderson, Charles Anderson, Arthur Thomas, and Arthur Lomand — arrived in Halifax via a motor boat from Main-à-Dieu. *Judique*, at seventy-four tons, was registered in Halifax.

Burning at LaHave River

Flames swept through the schooner *General Pau* in the early morning of May 25, 1930, as she lay at anchor at the mouth of the LaHave River, near Riverport Harbour.

A 329-ton tern, *General Pau* was built at Brooklyn in 1919 and registered to The Schooner General Pau Ltd. at Liverpool, Nova Scotia. In her years of coasting, she had sniffed the coastline extensively and the 122-foot-long vessel was well known.

In the fall of 1929, while returning to Nova Scotia from Turks Island with salt, she grounded at the mouth of the LaHave River with the local river pilot at the wheel. The following spring *General Pau*, under Captain J.C. MacKenzie of Halifax, was slated to be hauled out for repairs at the Meteghan shipyards; however, the fire completely destroyed the tern.

Two schooners in an autumn hurricane

When the schooner *Utilla* arrived in Yarmouth on September 7, 1930, Captain Oliver Comeau of Weymouth told of an horrific ordeal at sea. He claimed the 212-ton schooner was not built to withstand the terrific force of wind thrown at her.

Utilla had left Boston on July 16 for Turks Island and after a normal passage of fourteen days arrived and took on salt. On August 4, she set sail for Yarmouth and all went well until August 21; then Captain Comeau and his Nova Scotia crew encountered an easterly hurricane. For several hours the storm raged around the craft forcing the crew to take in all sail. *Utilla* was driven mercilessly before the wind under bare poles in mountainous seas. Waves repeatedly broke over the craft until the after cabin, galley and forecastle were flooded. Sea water found its way into the fresh water tanks, ruining the contents.

Fortunately *Utilla* had a small quantity of fresh water secure in another part of the schooner; had it not been for this meagre supply all on board would have died of thirst. The keg of water allowed the captain and crew one small drink each per day for fourteen days. The cook prepared meals with salt water. The high seas and wind, coupled with the damaged condition of all equipment and living spaces, made the experience of everyone aboard *Utilla* an adventure never to be forgotten.

Captain Comeau gave his position at sea while battling the gale as latitude 34.30, longitude 74.30. He had encountered the tail end of a southern hurricane. Although *Utilla* fought heavy seas all the way to Yarmouth, after the first gale abated, winds were relatively light.

Patricia Mary, a 52-ton Halifax schooner, was not so lucky. On September 7, the same day as *Utilla* sailed into port, she foundered fifteen miles off St. Paul's Island, northeast of the northern tip of Cape Breton. According to a message sent to C.H. Harvey, the provincial marine and fisheries agent, her crew landed safely on the island. At last report *Patricia Mary* was a drifting hulk, still afloat but waterlogged and a menace to navigation.

Beginning of the end

By the 1930s, with banking schooners becoming obsolete and unable to compete with modern trawlers, the traditional fish catching methods used by Nova Scotian schooners were being phased out. Many banking schooners lost at sea were not replaced, a few were converted to coasting vessels, and others were offered for sale at bargain prices.

As with fish processors in neighbouring Gloucester, Massachusetts, who had changed from the traditional hook and line catch and salt-dried preservation techniques, the Lunenburg and Shelburne fishing interests also modernized their fleets and purchased new trawlers. Trawlers caught more fish in less time, paid higher wages, and were safer since the men worked on the vessel rather than in small dories away from the mother ship. In time, Newfoundland would follow suit, but in the years between 1920 and 1940, the neighbouring island bought many of Nova Scotia's wooden bankers. Ads like the adjacent one appeared in local papers.

Those who controlled the salt fish industry and had shares in wooden schooners did not readi-

In *The Halifax Herald* of October 21, 1932, LaHave Outfitting has the banking schooner Vera P. Thornhill for sale, with or without fishing gear.

ly adapt to change. The United Maritime Fishermen of Halifax, Yarmouth, Shelburne and other traditional fishing ports protested in writing to the Prime Minister, R.B. Bennett, and E.N. Rhodes, Minister of Fisheries. The Nova Scotia fishermen complained against the granting of licenses to trawlers and urged the minister not to take a pro-trawler stand. Headlines in the *Sydney Post* of July 18, 1931, read "Trawlers Must Go, Fishermen Wire Bennett" and stated that: the fishermen's present methods are more modern than trawlers, which are undeniably destroying our fishing resources besides our social welfare; Canadian fishing grounds lie so near that trawlers are not essential to the industry; and the trawler fishery would spell doom to the fishermen of Nova Scotia.

One beam trawler manned by fifteen men could, the United Maritime Fishermen stated, catch as many fish as six fishing schooners each manned with twenty-four men; thus one trawler took away the earnings of 129 men. In 1930 there were forty-six schooners in the Lunenburg fleet which in 1931 declined to twenty. The beam trawler, the protest stated, had "strangled the Lockeport industry and the markets they once enjoyed were being supplied by trawlers."

With great foresight, the schooner fishermen predicted the end of the inshore fishing stocks saying: " . . . Where are the cod and haddock? Practically all the fish we catch on the western coast of Nova Scotia are taken from a few spasmodic night schools of fish, mostly pollock. Haddock, our luscious fish, in another ten years will be a thing of the past. Why? Because the drag net of the beam trawler is harrowing the ocean bed day and night, destroying the spawn, and millions of little fish too small for edible use are being thrown back into the sea. Does the public realize that thousands of cod and haddock in our adjacent waters are daily being destroyed in this way?"

The protest, signed by director Norman C. Sollows of United Maritime Fishermen, did little to stem the tide of beam trawlers. One by one wooden schooners disappeared, never to be seen again.

Still, as long as men went "down to the sea in ships and did business in great waters," the elements of danger remained. Although technology was changing the traditional mode of transportation on the sea and the methods of harvesting fish, death, disaster and major mishaps still occurred in the Nova Scotian fleet.

One of the first disasters to ravage the "beam trawlers" was the disappearance of *Jutland* in March 1920. Under the command of Captain Johnson, she left Lunenburg March 1 with twenty-one men. On March 11, the trawler *Lemberg* out of Halifax located a floating dory, badly smashed, full of water and with the body of *Jutland*'s mate, John R. Ellison. He had resided in Dartmouth. When a second dory, also damaged, was found some time later, owners and relatives realized she had come to a tragic end.

Lemberg sent word by wireless to Halifax then, while still in the vicinity where the dories had been found, steamed near a Gloucester trawler, *Walrus*. The Americans said they had passed *Jutland* the evening before, March 10, but had not heard or seen anything of her since then. Both vessels searched for wreckage, but found nothing.

Built at Liverpool, *Jutland* was put into commission for deep sea fishing in 1919. She had oil-burning engines which necessitated her coming to Halifax often for fuel, but she fished out of Liverpool. Some veteran fishermen believed that since she had an oil-burning engine, an explosion destroyed her; others maintained she was cut down by another ship. Today, one of Nova Scotia's first beam trawlers is posted as "Missing with crew." Her entire crew roster could not be located, but those listed are: Albert Backman and Bertram Creaser of Riverport; at least five from Liverpool, Allan Jollimore, Clarence Jollimore, John Jollimore, Frank Pitts, and Fred Selig; John Wolfe from Western Head; and Mcrae Crowell and John Macdonald of Port Joli.

Throughout the years other losses and disasters would strike the trawler fleet: for example, the sinking of *Good Hope* in March 1928 when all crewmen were saved; the crew of Liverpool's *Gladys Pauline*, commanded by Captain Scott, rescued April 25, 1974; the collision and sinking of Lunenburg's *Reliance* on June 17, 1966, with twelve men lost and four survivors still evokes sad memories.

General Page (above), a derelict at Shelburne. (Photo courtesy Captain Hubert Hall, Shipsearch Marine, Yarmouth)

Chapter 10 (1931-35)
Death of a salvage ship

Canusa: a Lunenburg story

The year 1931 was relatively free from shipping disasters: an American vessel, the 1,029-ton *Mary Bradford Pierce* stranded at Cape Smoky on July 17.

The Lunenburg schooner *Canusa* sank many miles from Nova Scotia. The circumstances of her sinking are, in part, derived from a story by J. Keith Young in *The Halifax Herald*, written twenty-eight years after the loss.

Seaworthy and powered by an engine, the schooner *Canusa*, under the command of Captain Joe Himmelman, left Lunenburg on September 25, 1931, destined for Puerto Rico with a cargo of dried fish. Fair winds and smooth seas graced the schooner on her voyage south. On October 7, when the cargo was discharged, she went to Turks Island for fishery salt.

Within two or three days this cargo was aboard and *Canusa* left for home. Himmelman put the vessel at half speed to allow the salt to settle. Then on October 10, the crew heard a loud retort or bang. Someone went below to investigate and came back with the bad news — the engine's drive shaft was broken and the wooden encasement (stuffing box) around it split. Water entered *Canusa* at an alarming rate. Heavily laden with salt, Himmelman knew the schooner would settle in the water; thus he ordered all men to the pumps.

Somehow the shaft was repaired and the schooner got underway, but water rose rapidly. To make matters worse, the east-southeast wind had increased in intensity to gale force. *Canusa* wallowed sluggishly. At 5:30 a.m. on October 13 all hands reported on deck in an effort to lighten and to repair the schooner. But despite working all day through the October cold and wind, Captain Himmelman and his crew knew *Canusa* was doomed and had to be abandoned.

Himmelman, in an interview with *The Halifax Herald*, described his preparations to abandon ship: "Time as well as the ocean was the enemy and all hands began to make sails for the [three] dories. Two blankets sufficed for one sail while another was made from two tablecloths. Materials were exhausted and one dory left when the idea of using old straw sacks proved to be satisfactory. Food, water, and other needful things were packed and without more ado, we left the sinking ship at six a.m. on October 15. Sail was set and the ill-assorted pod of tiny boats left for San Salvador, some 153 miles distant."

The next day the wind veered around southwest. The crewmen, each taking his turn, manned the oars for twenty-eight hours. Soon their hands blistered from the prolonged pull at the oars. A fair breeze gave them respite from rowing and late on the evening of the eighteenth, they sighted the purple smudge of land in the distance — San Salvador!

But fortunes reversed. The wind died and the weary crew shipped the oars again. That night, when the dories were six miles from land, the fickle wind swung to the north and a sudden squall of wind and rain separated the boats. Up to this time, aided by the light of a lantern by night and by sight at day they had kept together. Now increased winds extinguished the lanterns as soon as they were lit. From Captain Himmelman's view, one dory was thought to be headed for shore but he doubted it could land safely. The coastline was unknown to them and could have reefs and rocks. Wind increased and the night was heavy with thunder and lightning.

As Himmelman claimed later, "It was the worst time I spent in a dory in eighteen years experience." Blinding lightning lit the final four miles to land. Himmelman's dory crashed onto the reef, but the men kept her away from other rocks and headed for shore. The other dory had already landed and its men held up their lantern to guide the way. The third dory hung offshore until daylight and it too made land safely.

The Herald described what happened to *Canusa*'s crew: "Morning saw the bedraggled men cheered by a dog's bark and natives [of San Salvador] who appeared minutes later. They immediately provided food and shelter. *Canusa*'s crew remained on the eastern side of the island for two days. They then went across to the west side where the Governor took care of the crew. A few days later the men hailed the mail boat and went to Nassau arriving on the 24th of October and remained there a day."

The shipwrecked crew joined the vessel *Lady Rodney* headed to Montreal and arrived there November 2. Finally the last leg of their long journey home began when they boarded the train for Lunenburg. On November 4 they again set foot in their hometown — a total of thirty-five days had elapsed.

Death of Nova Scotian salvage ship — *Sandbeach*

The wreck of *His Majesty's Ship Raleigh* on August 8, 1922, is a frequently told story of shipwreck and drowning on Newfoundland's shores. Not so well known is the disaster surrounding *Sandbeach*, a Nova Scotia-based tug involved in the salvage of *Raleigh*'s remains in 1932.

With her stern below waterline, *HMS Raleigh*, lies stranded and a rusting hulk at Point Amour in the Strait of Belle Isle. The ill-fated *Sandbeach* salvaged her valuable metals. (Courtesy Marine Archives, St. John's, Capt. Harry Stone Collection)

Raleigh, a 12,000-ton cruiser in the British navy, visited Corner Brook in August of 1922 and then proceeded to steam to the Labrador coast. As she travelled north through the Strait of Belle Isle, a combination of fog, icebergs and faulty navigation put *Raleigh* on the rocks near the Point Amour lighthouse.

Raleigh's crew salvaged several small and easily transported items from the wreck, then she was left for residents of the area to take what they could. In 1926 the vessel *Stanhill* carried a demolition team to Point Amour to complete the damage begun by the sea and those looking for salvage. When *Stanhill*'s work was completed and *Raleigh*'s remains were scattered on the seabed, she carried seven of *Raleigh*'s fifteen-inch guns to Halifax.

T.F. & M. Salvaging and Wrecking Company, whose agents were W.A. Murray of New York City, made one of the final attempts at large-scale salvage of *H.M.S. Raleigh*. It was an ill-prepared undertaking. The ship chartered to do the work was S.S. *Sandbeach*, based in Halifax. *Sandbeach* left Halifax on September 25, 1932, went directly to the wreck site, and prepared to gather salvage from the bottom and shoreline.

Built in Thompkins Cove, New York, *Sandbeach* was a wooden screw steamer of 248 tons, single-decked, and measured 119 feet long and 9.3 feet deep. She was owned by Rockaway White Sand Company and registered in New York.

Captain B.M. Moody of New Brunswick was in charge of the ship while Lieutenant J.A. Tardiff represented the British navy. Other crew members were: cook Andrew Berg, Saskatchewan; Rene and Antoine Bouchard, St. François, Quebec; chief engineer G.J. (Thomas) Shortt, Oscar Bennett, James McCall, G. Butt, all of Halifax; Gus and Wilfred Sampson, Nova Scotia; and John Costigan of Colliers, Newfoundland.

Salvage was great. Using divers, floating platforms and explosives, the professional wreckers aboard *Sandbeach* took a full load to Corner Brook, a stopover port for fuel as *Sandbeach* headed for Halifax and New York.

In early December, when *Sandbeach* arrived in Corner Brook, her owners were slapped with a court summons by the Newfoundland Railway. Apparently the salvage company owed for coal, crew's wages and demurrage — money owed from failure to load or discharge on time. The case came before the Supreme Court in Admiralty in St. John's and, on an order from the court, *Sandbeach* was released.

Through a twist of fate, the proceedings of the brief court trial cost Captain Moody his life. Both he and R.S. Grant, who represented the salvage company, bought tickets at the St. John's railway station and were preparing to leave for Corner Brook. R. Gushue, legal counsel for T.F. & M. Salvaging, suggested Grant stay over in case he was needed in any further proceedings. Captain Moody used his ticket in a fateful rendezvous with the S.S. *Sandbeach* awaiting at Corner Brook.

Those who recalled *Sandbeach's* departure from Corner Brook remembered her as very heavily laden, not only with material from the hulk of *Raleigh* but from wrecking equipment and a considerable quantity of explosives.

At this point, the final tragic scene of the tale of *Sandbeach* changes to a small uninhabited stretch of shore, Little Friars Cove, about twelve miles west of Highlands and sixty miles southwest of Corner Brook on Newfoundland's West Coast. The date: December 5, 1932. Clues to a sea mystery had to be pieced together from debris and mutilated bodies.

Two men from Highlands, John Flynn and Richard McEachern, who knew nothing of *Sandbeach* or her activities, discovered a lifeboat and the body of a dead man on the beach in Little Friars Cove on Monday evening, December 5. They found two life belts on the beach, one considerably blood stained. The dead body bore no scars and the men assumed the blood belonged to another seaman. They reported that the name on the lifeboat was "S.S. Sandbeach" and it had drifted in sometime Sunday night or Monday morning.

The seventeen-foot lifeboat was bottom up in the landwash and the body nearby, face down on the sand. The dead man was about 175 pounds in weight, around thirty-five years of age and evidently had been in a hurry to leave the ship. He was dressed in an ordinary lounge suit with a white shirt, low shoes and rubbers. It seemed as if he had died on the shore.

One oar, but no food, was found in the lifeboat and others might have been in the lifeboat as the row-locks had been used. The grisly discovery was found in a small cove surrounded by towering cliffs and scarcely any beach. The nearest law authority, Constable Dawe at St. Fintan's, who had been told of the gruesome find, ordered no one to touch the evidence despite the fact that a high tide or waves might wash the body out to sea. News spread through the West Coast towns of Highlands, St. Fintan's, Maidstones, and Heatherton, but no one knew of a missing ship nor the identity of the seaman.

That same evening at seven o'clock another body was picked up at Fischells. He seemed about sixty years of age and the only identification items within his clothes were a knife, a key-wind watch and personal papers, one a letter addressed to Captain B.M. Moody. On December 9, it was determined the remains were those of Captain Moody and his body was sent to New Brunswick for burial.

From that evidence the ship and crew were soon positively identified. In the next days more proof that the S.S. *Sandbeach* and her crew had come to a quick and fatal end appeared at Heatherton, a small town a few miles northeast of Highlands. Shattered wreckage found along the shore included broken parts of a wheel, pieces of decking, part of a cabin and several lifebuoys. Within two days two more bodies with the marks of scalding, apparently from steam, on the arms and faces were discovered.

In the following weeks the Newfoundland Justice Department initiated an enquiry headed by Magistrate O'Rielly of St. George's. By December 23, 1932, the report of the loss of *Sandbeach* concluded: "It is the opinion of the Court the *Sandbeach* was destroyed by an explosion. The shattered wreckage . . . point to the conclusion. In addition there were marks of scalding from steam on the corpses . . . but death was due from drowning." [The more graphic details of mutilation have been deleted.]

Richard Grase, the supercargo of S.S. *Sandbeach*, who supervised the cargo and loading but had not sailed on the missing vessel, identified the ship, her cargo and the bodies. In his evidence Grase thought that the clothing indicated the men had left the ship in a hurry. Abrasions, cuts, scalds and broken bones signified that some of the crew had been struck with flying objects and steam. According to Grase's testimony, the steamship had been carrying nine full cases and three broken cases of dynamite. This was stored near the engine room in the lazarette, or the afterpart of a ship's hold used for stores. No concrete proof could be established as to exactly where or when an explosion destroyed the S.S. *Sandbeach* and her crew.

The body found on the shore at Fischells was that of the captain; the two at Heatherton were Shortt and Sampson. The boat which drifted in at Little Friars Cove contained the body of the cook, Andrew Berg. Presumably the body of Costigan, the Newfoundland sailor aboard *Sandbeach*, was not found.

At the enquiry, McEachern and Flynn, farmers of Highlands, described the difficulty they had in recovering Berg's body and in getting it to St. George's. They enlisted the help of six other men. On Wednesday, two days after discovery, using ropes they lifted Berg's remains up over a 700-foot cliff, then tied the body in canvas and brought it on their shoulders to Paul's Gulch, a distance of eight miles. From there the corpse was transported by boat to Highlands, then carried by horse and cart to St. Fintan's and finally put on a train to St. George's. Their work took from Wednesday to Saturday with the most difficult section from Little Friars Cove to Paul's Gulch, an uninhabited and remote section of the coast. They had to blaze and practically make a trail through virgin woods and brush, sleeping in improvised shelters as they went.

Thus, after the enquiry report, the snippets of a sea disaster and bits of news surrounding its mysterious end, the steamship *Sandbeach* faded from local papers. Today her remains, as well as the valuable fittings, brass, copper and salvage of *HMS Raleigh*, lie somewhere on the ocean's bottom between Highlands and Fischells.

Remains of a wreck at Drum Head

Finding the mute evidence of a shipwreck was not confined to foreign shores. The discovery of casks of cod liver oil on September 21, 1932, off Drum Head indicated some vessel had been in trouble or was lost. Drum Head is located on Nova Scotia's Eastern Shore, south of Cape Canso. Fishermen found three casks — two filled with cod liver oil, the other with water — and most surprisingly a dory marked *L.A. Dunton*, a fishing schooner out of Gloucester, Massachusetts.

When authorities contacted Gloucester, it was learned that *Patara*, one of Gloucester's last all-sail schooners, was overdue and had indeed carried dories from *L.A. Dunton*, a Gloucester banking schooner, on deck. *Patara*, built in Mahone Bay in 1921, was used first in the fishery and then for rum-running. As a rum-runner she was apprehended by the US Coast Guard and taken to New York, where she was purchased by Captain Ben Pine and the Atlantic Supply Company. Under Pine she was engaged in strictly legal business — fishing. Pine was a frequent rival of

Captain Angus Walters and the *Bluenose* for the International Fisherman's Trophy.

On August 13, skippered by Captain Matthew L. Critchell of Bucksport, Maine (and formerly of Belleoram, Newfoundland), *Patara* sailed from Gloucester for Domino Run, Labrador. There she loaded salt fish and 105 barrels of cod liver oil and left for Gloucester on September 3, but due to strong winds was forced in to Long Point, Quebec. On September 7 she left, but then seemed to disappear for no one could account for her whereabouts. A gale had swept Cape Breton around September 9-11 and only this could explain *Patara's* disappearance.

Upon receiving the news of debris off Nova Scotia, Captain Pine stated: "She is one of the last New England schooners depending on canvas alone. She had been re-rigged, caulked and outfitted with a new suit of sail before she left Gloucester. She should withstand that recent gale so I am not giving her up yet."

But more evidence of *Patara's* loss came when the British steamer *Hazelwood* passed the wooden superstructure of a schooner off southern Labrador. That helped confirmed her fate; American newspapers on October 7 declared, "Give up Overdue Sch. Patara as Lost."

Patara carried six crewmen and, according to owner Ben Pine, a "guest." Just before *Patara* left on her last voyage, a young man named Arthur Schmidt, aged 18, asked permission to sail on the schooner. He told Pine he was on vacation and his home was in San Francisco. This was confirmed by Pine who, in mid-September, received a telegram from the boy's mother asking if he had sailed on the schooner. He wired back saying the boy had sailed on *Patara*. Now Pine was faced with reporting his death at sea as well as the loss of the other six men: Critchell, aged 48, William Delaney, James F. Hallett, Francis Lloyd, John Rose, and Philip Mason, all listed as living in or near Gloucester.

It was as if *Patara*, built on the shores of Nova Scotia, had returned home for her final hours. As well, *Patara's* loss mirrored the disappearance of the renown Gloucester sailer *Columbia*, which vanished with all hands near Sable Island (see Chapter 9). With the loss of both schooners, only two of Gloucester's great sailing fleet remained — *Thomas Gorton* and *Elsie*, the latter a competitor in the sailing race for the International Fisherman's Trophy.

But *Patara* was not the only bad news for Nova Scotians in September 1932. Fears arose for the whereabouts of the schooner *Bee Bee* captained by Bartholemew (Bart) B. Dunphy, a brother of vessel owner and merchant Sylvester Dunphy of North Sydney.

Bee Bee, named for the initials of her captain, was known to be off the coast of Cape Breton during the September 10 gale. According to local knowledge, she had been involved in the rum-running trade; her last port of departure was St. Pierre where she had taken on a load of liquour. A small vessel, *Bee Bee* (or *Be Be* as she was known in St. Pierre) carried two or three crew believed to be young men from the French islands. *Bee Bee* was known to be without gasoline; thus it was thought that with no engine power she would have been blown out to sea and would take several days to sail back to land. Patrol boats sent to search the seas off Cape Breton returned without sighting *Bee Bee* or the crew.

A memorial stone to Captain Dunphy in St. Peter's Catholic Church Cemetery in Ingonish, Cape Breton, reads: "Dunphy, Bartholemew B., D. Sept 10 1932 at 33 yrs. old, lost at sea."

Evidence of a wreck at Cranberry Head

When the Newfoundland schooner *Bessie McDonald* was forced to return to North Sydney due to a September 23 storm, she reported sighting the spars of a vessel sticking out of the water three miles northeast of Cranberry Head. *Bessie McDonald* with her load of Sydney coal, had left North Sydney on Friday, September 23, 1932, encountered heavy weather, returned and reported the sunken derelict.

On September 24, Nova Scotian shipping authorities sent Captain Croft and the

RUM VESSEL IS MISSING OFF COAST

Schooner Bee Bee Feared Lost in Cape Breton Storm Last Week-End

NORTH SYDNEY, Sept. 21 — The schooner Bee Bee, Captain Bart Dunphy, of Ingonish, C. B., which was off the coast during the recent

This is how *The Halifax Herald* reported the loss of the *Bee Bee* on September 22, 1932. Eventually she was posted as "Lost with crew."

revenue cutter *Adversus* to the area to ascertain the exact position and identity of the wreck. The crew attached a rope to the spars and began towing when the line snapped. On Monday the tug *Lady Laurier* made a line fast, but again the line broke. It was determined the hulk had the remains of a heavy cargo in her holds. As well, the spars showed evidence of having been underwater for some time; thus veteran seamen felt sure the wreck was the schooner *Vera E. Himmelman*, a 93-ton schooner owned in Lunenburg. With Captain Trenholme in command, *Vera E. Himmelman* had left North Sydney more than two years previously headed for Bras d'Or Lake. She foundered on April 12, 1930 between Cranberry Head and Point Aconi with no loss of life.

On October 25, 1933, hope for the safety of the 400-ton, steel-hulled *Dorin* (above) was abandoned. Her owner, Captain John T. Cruickshank, whose younger brother was a crewman aboard, said, " . . . she was an old auxiliary schooner, a veteran of many battles with the elements, and has succumbed at last to the deep." *Dorin*, based out of Yarmouth, was last seen leaving Nassau, Bahamas, on September 10, 1933, with salt from Turks Island.

In the same time period two other Nova Scotian sailing ships were missing and feared lost with their crews. *Cape Blomidon*, out of Parrsboro and overdue from New York to Yarmouth, carried a crew of seven men and a cargo of coal. Two days after she left New York on October 23, 1933, a vicious storm swept the Atlantic coast. The seas had hardly quieted when another northeaster battered the seas. *Ena F. Parsons*, a Parrsboro schooner, was dismasted and overturned. Her derelict hull was located and towed ashore, but no bodies of crewmen were found.

A premature August Gale, North Sydney

August was yet two days away and there was no precedent for a "July Gale"; accordingly boat owners around North Sydney described the intense storm that arrived without warning in the late hours of July 30, 1935, as a "premature August Gale." It whipped into North Sydney harbour in a fury causing damage among the small craft berthed at local docks. Accompanied by driving rain, the gale had skippers and owners increasing mooring lines and securing sail. Two small craft broke moorings and were only retrieved after considerable trouble. At Sydney Mines a plate glass window at Woolworth's store blew in at the height of the storm.

Shiloh, registered at Lunenburg and owned by her captain, Joseph Best, ran into the storm while beating her way into North Sydney from the fishing grounds. She hit the jagged Petrie's Ledge forcing Best and his crew of four to abandon ship and make for shore. Captain Best, feeling his vessel could be salvaged, intended to row out and assess damage to the 22-ton craft.

By the next day, July 31, Best had the unpleasant task of reporting to the police that not only was *Shiloh* wrecked, but she had been ransacked as she lay on the rocks. Someone had gone out to the stranded schooner and looted items, including parts of the auxiliary engine, from her deck and holds.

Shiloh, with her side broken open, lay on her beam ends as Best, his crew and local Sydney men removed fishing gear, rigging, and seventy-nine gallons of gasoline. The salvage was brought to North Sydney on Captain Thomas Hardy's schooner, *Augustus Gordon*.

Hurry On survivors reach Judique

A suitcase washed ashore two miles north of Judique, Cape Breton, another tragic reminder of the treacherous sea. It belonged to Fraser MacLean of Pictou Island, one of five victims on a motor vessel which foundered in September 1935.

The steamer *Hurry On* left Halifax on Sunday, September 22, 1935, for Montreal. Off Port Hood Island a heavy gale battered the ship. *Hurry On*, tossed like a cork in mountainous seas, listed out when her cargo

Hurry On (the dark-hulled steamer, centre), owned by the Unis Shipping Company, was well known around the shipping ports of Nova Scotia. In September 1935, she capsized and five of her crew perished. In this photo she navigates through winter ice at Canso in company with *Robert G. Cann* (left), the vessel which helped rescue the crew of *Margaretville* in 1925. On February 16, 1946, *Robert G. Cann* foundered at Tiverton, Bay of Fundy, and twelve lives were lost. The *Nova IV* is to the right of *Hurry On*. (Photo courtesy Public Archives of Nova Scotia)

shifted. When the list reached thirty-five degrees Captain Gardiner ordered his crew of eleven to abandon ship; true to the tradition of the sea, the captain was the last to leave. Three minutes after the crew left, she fell on her side and slid to the bottom.

For twenty-four hours, battling high winds, seas, and cold, the twelve headed for land in the open lifeboat. Fraser MacLean, aged 38, died of exposure soon after getting into the boat and three other men perished that long night: Captain E.H. Gardiner, aged 60 of Halifax, married; third engineer James MacAulay, 24, River Denys; and donkeyman Alexander Waye, 18, of Vancouver. Their bodies were swept into the churning seas by huge waves washing over the lifeboat.

The remaining eight survivors reached land on the shores of St. George's Bay, about a half mile from the town of Judique. While attempting to land, mate William MacKenzie, 30, of Upper Leitche's Creek, Cape Breton, drowned when the lifeboat capsized. Again heroism in the face of overwhelming odds came through when second engineer Boudrot, although cold and exhausted himself, dived under the overturned craft to pull the ship's cook, Joe Gapargo, to safety.

First reports of the disaster came at nine o'clock Tuesday morning, September 24. Two of *Hurry On*'s crew limped into the home of William MacDonald, told him of the tragedy and asked that medical help be summoned right away for the rest of the crew still at the beach. Residents of Judique then hastened to the shoreline to find MacLean's lifeless body in the battered and oarless boat. Five other men were in weak condition.

Immediately someone communicated with Inverness and Port Hood. Medical personnel rushed to Judique and soon the shipwrecked survivors were in St. Mary's Hospital, Inverness. D.J. MacDonald, a merchant of North Sydney and nurse Mrs. Duncan McLellan, formerly of the Kentville Sanatorium, helped move the castaways to Inverness. *Hurry On*'s chief engineer Herman developed pneumonia, but pulled through his ordeal. The survivors were: H.H. Herman, 32; Alexander Boudrot, 30; Jack Evans, 28; Herman Baker, 27; Joe Gapargo, 35, all of Halifax; Gus Carmichael, 23, of St. Ann's, Cape Breton; and Gilbert Boyd, 18, of Truro.

By September 27 a search by local schooners had failed to find any trace of the other victims. A Mounted Police plane dispatched from Sydney, three planes from the Cape Breton Flying Club led by instructor Lindsay Rood, and a vessel from Port Hawksbury aided in the search.

M.W. Colp (above at Digby), a 36-ton schooner registered in Lunen-burg, sank on June 1, 1940, four miles southwest of Grimes Bay, Nova Scotia. (Photo courtesy C.F. McBride and Shipsearch Marine, Captain Hubert Hall, Yarmouth)

D.J. Thornhill on the stocks in Grand Bank, Newfoundland, in September 1935. A Nova Scotian master shipbuilder, Hughie McKay, oversaw the work. Captain John Thornhill had asked McKay's Shipyards at Shelburne, Nova Scotia, to send someone to Grand Bank to build his schooner. McKay, aged 21, arrived in early summer and left when *D.J. Thornhill* was launched on November 26, 1935. (Photo courtesy Otto Kelland and Hughie McKay, master builder)

Chapter 11 (1936–41)
Disaster in Halifax harbour

Rescue at Point Aconi

On October 18, 1936, the Newfoundland schooner *Louis A. Conrad* foundered at Point Aconi, fifteen miles northeast of Sydney. Captain William Kearley and his crew of five — Billy and Harry Kearley, Levi Savoury, George Mullins of Belleoram, and Edgar Reid of Harbour Buffett — were sighted by the banker *Haligonian*. *Haligonian*'s skipper sent out a dory crew who approached the stranded schooner. Captain Kearley, reluctant to leave the craft he was fond of, refused to board the dory and practically had to be pulled aboard. A 45-mile-an-hour gale forced *Louis A. Conrad* onto the rocks. Within hours the schooner was reduced to debris along the shoreline.

Halifax harbour collision: *Flirt* and *Marshall Frank*

Looming out of the blackness of a night laced with patches of coastal fog, the 100-ton motorized schooner *Marshall Frank* knifed through the fishing vessel *Flirt*. In a matter of minutes, *Flirt* was kindling. Of the six fishermen aboard *Flirt*, four escaped with their lives but Captain Jake Weymouth and Lance Locke disappeared with the sunken vessel.

In the darkest hour of 4:30 a.m. on Monday, March 15, 1937, as the little *Flirt* lay to near Halifax harbour, she was struck just aft of the main rigging. *Marshall Frank*, running at eight and a half knots, rammed the Halifax fishing vessel, which was stopped in the harbour fairway just inside Chebucto Head, as the crew prepared for a day of fishing.

Most of the six crewmen were on the deck of their small vessel baiting trawls and upon impact were thrown into the sea. The last glimpse the four survivors had of Captain Weymouth was when he was trying to move his craft to avert disaster. He was still at the wheel of *Flirt* when last seen. Locke, the cook, was below deck.

Captain Jake Weymouth, aged 41, was born in Molliers, a now abandoned community on the west side of Newfoundland's Burin Peninsula. After his wife died in the 1930s, Weymouth chose to make a living in Halifax and found employment on *Flirt*, owned by Bentley and Flemming Ltd. of Halifax who had purchased the vessel from Captain Edward O'Neill, Halifax. Weymouth lived aboard *Flirt*.

Lance Locke, born in Trinity, Newfoundland, had lived in Halifax for eleven years. He had been employed on the Halifax-based trawler *Viernoe* and joined *Flirt* two years before. His brother Richard, employed as a shoemaker, lived on Chebucto Road and another brother Levi sailed on the cable ship *Lord Kelvin*. Locke's sister, Mrs. Freeman Butler, resided on Monaghan Lane, Halifax.

Flirt's other four crewmen were rescued: John Hanlon and David O'Hearn of Canso, Nova Scotia, and two Newfoundlanders, Jerome Farrell of Bay de Nord in Fortune Bay, and Joseph Savoury who belonged to Parsons Harbour.

The impact of *Marshall Frank*'s hit was so heavy and direct the fishing vessel was smashed to pieces. Moments after the crash all that remained was drifting wreckage. Shrill cries of men pleading for help filled the blackness of the night, but the search for survivors was hampered by patches of fog. Lights flashing from the Lunenburg banker revealed tragic scenes of men fighting to keep afloat in the harbour amid broken planks, trawl tubs, dories, oars, and debris.

Marshall Frank's captain, Frank Risser, one of the best known of Lunenburg's fishing skippers, directed the rescue work. Risser was in the

On February 17, 1949, *Marshall Frank* (above), a 144-ton banker owned by James Petite of Halifax, stranded on Marie Joseph Shoals off Nova Scotia during a severe winter storm. She had been built in Lunenburg's Smith and Rhuland yards in 1926. (Photo courtesy C.F. McBride and Hubert Hall, Shipsearch Marine, Yarmouth)

wheelhouse when the collision occurred. *Marshall Frank*, owned and based in Lunenburg, was inbound from the fishing banks off Halifax harbour. In the collision, she had nine stanchions broken off on the starboard bow. "I saw no lights and did not know the *Flirt* was on our course until we struck," Captain Risser asserted. The helmsman, Carl Wagner of Lunenburg, also said there were no lights showing from the sunken vessel.

When they were brought to shore, the survivors related their stories of narrow escapes from drowning. John Hanlon said: "I could not swim a stroke. I went under water. It seemed a long time and I gave up hope. Then I came to the surface. There was some wreckage by me and I managed to take a hold and keep afloat until I was picked up in a dory."

Savoury and Farrell were rescued in a like manner. Both said they would have quickly sunk to the bottom, weighted down by heavy sea boots and oilskins, but for wreckage which kept them afloat.

Only one of *Flirt*'s crew, David O'Hearn, succeeded in climbing over *Marshall Frank*'s rail. He stated: "When the crash came, I leaped and grasped the rail and tried to pull myself over it. There was some wreckage being carried along by the schooner's bow and I clung to that. The wreckage began slipping astern and I kept trying to crawl aboard. Then hands grasped me from the deck and helped me reach the schooner's deck."

Marshall Frank's crew jumped from their bunks after the ramming and raced topside to help. The engines were reversed immediately and dories put over the side instantly. One was manned by Ronald Mossman, P. Smith and Lepine Mosher. Helmsman Carl Wagner, Russell Hirtic and Willis Mosher rowed out in another. The first dory to the site rescued John Hanlon and the second pulled Joseph Savoury from the water. Ten minutes later the last of those rescued was taken aboard. Despite a long and thorough search no trace was found of Weymouth and Locke.

When *Marshall Frank* docked at Halifax Fisheries Company its flag flew at half-mast, signalling the end of an unfortunate trip for the big schooner. She also had only 55,000 pounds of fish to show for a week out on the banks.

Twelve years later *Marshall Frank* was wrecked at Framboise Cove; this time the loss of life was greater when five Newfoundland fishermen died. (See the story of her final hours in Chapter 12.)

Hebridean: Halifax and Herring Cove

By 1940 the busy port of Halifax, with its large and deep natural harbour, was called upon to furnish the greatest effort in its history. During World War Two, it became the transshipment port for troops, tons of arms, supplies, and food destined for war-torn Europe. Large convoys gathered in Bedford Basin in preparation for the hazardous voyage across the Atlantic. Ships entering and leaving the busy harbour did so under the guidance of pilot boats.

When the wreck of Pilot Boat Number Two, *Hebridean*, occurred on the night of March 28, 1940, it was the worst blow to the Halifax harbour pilotage system in its 150-year history. Rammed by an incoming freighter, the pilot boat sank like a stone and no bodies were ever found.

Hebridean (above) was a two-masted wooden vessel built in Lunenburg County in 1928. In 1940, while serving as a pilot boat, she was rammed and sank near Halifax harbour resulting in the death of nine men. (Photo C.F. McBride and Shipsearch Marine, Capt. Hubert Hall, Yarmouth)

That March night was clear and calm. A British freighter approached Halifax harbour and, as required by law and custom, had to be piloted or guided in. James Renner, in charge of *Hebridean*, manoeuvred the pilot boat near the large freighter. A few minutes before midnight, pilot Tupper Hayes, bosun Walter Power and Edward MacLaughlin, all of Halifax, put off in a tender — the little craft engaged in transferring the pilots — from *Hebridean* so that Hayes could board the freighter. Just as Hayes was about to do so, the freighter and the *Hebridean* collided.

The sharp steel prow of the freighter severed *Hebridean* in two and the pilot boat sank within a minute. The impact also overturned the tender and plunged its three occupants into the water. Immediately the freighter lowered its lifeboat and the searchers located Roy Sullivan of Halifax and Captain Carl Himmelman swimming in the icy water. Both had been hurled off *Hebridean*. Hayes, Power, and MacLaughlin were soon rescued and taken on board the freighter. Other crewmen and pilots of *Hebridean* would not be found and were presumed drowned, trapped inside the pilot boat during the collision. A Halifax tug, *Samson* under Captain Dykeman, went to the scene but found nothing.

Although first reported as a victim, pilot Edward Renner, a resident of 67 Larch Street, Halifax, escaped. An hour or so earlier he had stepped off *Hebridean* to steer another vessel into the harbour. James Renner, who was on *Hebridean* was probably crushed at the wheel.

Three experienced pilots — brothers Carleton and James Dempsey and their cousin Lorne Dempsey — disappeared in the wreckage. They had been ashore in Herring Cove earlier in the day and joined the pilot boat for their evening's work.

In Halifax the tragedy pervaded everyone's mind and discussion, but no one could explain exactly what had happened. Captain N. Lamont Power, a pilot who two hours before had joined a ship which he had guided into the harbour, could only say: "Despite the bright night and calm sea, a thousand and one things could have caused the collision. I don't feel like going out into the harbour again. I will always picture myself sailing over the bodies of those men. They were good, thoroughly trained pilots who can't be replaced."

The steamer had escaped damage, but there was no sign of the wreckage of the pilot boat. Superintendent of the pilots, Captain D.A. Reside stated the lights of *Hebridean* were working and that the radiophone had been repaired. He had been communicating with her around eleven p.m.

Such was the dire need and shortage of experienced pilots in Halifax harbour that Tupper Hayes, who had nearly been killed in the collision, reported for duty on *Nauphila*, Pilot Boat Number One, the day after the accident. (*Nauphila*'s story appears in Chapter 12.) When asked about the cause, Hayes could only reply that in the dark he could see nothing and had no idea what had happened. Sullivan and Himmelman could not report for work. Suffering from shock and exposure, they were brought to the Halifax Infirmary where Doctor K.P. Hayes feared that they had contracted pneumonia.

In addition to pilot Renner and the three Dempsey men, others killed in the mishap were engineer Matthew Power and Lawrence Thomas, both of Herring Cove, bosun Roy Purcell of Portuguese Cove, pilot Lionel Pelham of Halifax, and Claude Martin.

On April 6 while still in hospital, Captain Carl Himmelman, a 42-year-old master mariner born in LaHave, spoke of his ordeal saying, "I had my hands on the squid [little lifeboat] to launch it, but the rigging of my sinking ship came down over my shoulder." He then jumped into the sea. "I was never under water so long in my life. I kept thinking if only I could hold my breath long enough to get back to the surface. After I jumped into the water, I picked up a small piece of wood, placed it across my chest, held it there with one hand and paddled with the other."

For a half hour he struggled to stay afloat in the cold water while listening to others thrashing around him. Many of those thrown from *Hebridean* survived until minutes before a rescue boat would have reached their side. Himmelman, a former Lunenburg skipper, continued: "I saw them and heard them shouting all around me after the pilot boat sank. Some didn't last very long, but many stayed up quite a while. I picked up this stick — only a small piece of wood — but it kind of gave me security and courage. I almost gave up a half dozen times. I thought it would help me as long as I held on to it.

"When I saw the lifeboat from the freighter being launched, I tried to shout but I couldn't speak. Then all of a sudden something like a second strength came to me and my voice came back and got louder and louder. I saw the boat going over to where I had heard Roy Sullivan shouting, about a quarter mile away. . . . When the boat finally did come to me, I was picked out of the water. I remember being taken to the side of the steamer. A rope was put around me to lift me up, but after that it's all a blank until I came to with Dr. Hayes standing beside me."

The only wreckage found of *Hebridean* was located four days after she sank. Her fog horn, which had rested in the radio room at the stern of the pilot craft, drifted into Grand Desert approximately ten miles away. Alfred LaPierre, a Grand Desert fishermen, brought the fifty-pound device into the Halifax Pilotage Office where pilot Emmett DeLouchery identified it.

Days after the accident, flags at Halifax, Herring Cove and other towns flew at half-mast. The loss of experienced men in wartime when they were most needed was difficult and that was coupled with the personal loss of families. Today a memorial plaque hangs in St. Paul's Church, Herring Cove, where many of *Hebridean*'s victims were born or resided.

Parrsboro schooner wrecked

Winter took a tight grip on Nova Scotia on the weekend of April 19-21, 1940 — snow, rain and sleet driven by a heavy gale. Vessels off Nova Scotia's coast sought shelter where they could. Those with men and ships at sea rested uneasily.

One vessel, out of Parrsboro, was too small to withstand the onslaught of winter conditions. It was the 84-ton *Vida A*, built in 1922 at Port Greville for Oliver Allen and owned by Rufus Huntley. Huntley had bought *Vida A* from Captain James Ogilvie in 1939 and used her primarily for carrying coal from Parrsboro to Black's Harbour, New Brunswick. *Vida A* was classed as an auxiliary schooner since she had an engine but could also rely on her sails for power.

When the gale increased she lost her sails and fell helpless when her engine gave out. While trying to make Dipper Harbour, twenty-five miles down the coast from Saint John, Captain William Hill and his crew (mate Fred Legere and cook Onslow Legere) realized they could not keep *Vida A* off the rocks. In the blinding snowstorm, she struck the shoals as dawn was breaking on April 21. One of the crew placed a plank from the schooner to a rock and by this precarious means he crawled to land. Then he threw a rope to the other two, who followed the plank and rope to salvation.

Captain Hill and his two shipmates turned to look at *Vida A* only to see her break up. The top half, decks and upper structure, floated away while the bottom remained on the rocks. A few hours later all that could be seen was the top of one mast showing above water. The three men walked to Musquash, nine miles from Dipper Harbour, to phone concerned loved ones and then returned to Dipper Harbour for the night. *Vida A*'s former captain, James Legere, had had to leave the vessel the week before when he broke his arm at Apple River.

With the loss of *Vida A*, an era was coming to an end — now only one of this type of vessel, a wooden schooner powered by sail and motor, was left on the Nova Scotia–Bay of Fundy trade.

One of Sweeney's fleet, the 95-ton *Princess Pat* (above) went aground at Flat Mud Island, Bay of Fundy, on November 29, 1949. She was built in 1930 and served her owners well, having tirelessly delivered general cargo and coal around the coast. (Photo courtesy Yarmouth County Historical Society)

Fire off Halifax

Life on the sea poses many perils to sailors and ships: collision, stranding, storms, but one of the most terrifying dangers is fire. Fire, fanned by wind from the ship's forward motion, quickly consumes a wooden ship; in iron-hulled steamers fumes, gas and fuel give flames rapid headway.

Sailors faced with a shipboard fire have two immediate concerns — to fight the blaze and to save their lives should an uncontrollable fire force them to abandon ship. The ship has to be stopped or slowed to get lifeboats off properly and if the blaze is in the engine room, shutting down engines is difficult or impossible. Fire aboard a ship is a dreaded enemy from which there seems no easy escape.

Such was the situation off Halifax on March 26, 1941, when flames enveloped *HMCS Otter*. High winds, the raging Atlantic, and a rapid, uncontrollable inferno mitigated against *Otter's* crew. One event which eased the situation somewhat was the timely arrival of other ships, but in the end nearly half the crew lost their lives.

One of the first ships to arrive on the scene of the burning *Otter* was a merchant ship (not identified in reports), engaged in bringing supplies into and out of Halifax. Her skipper described what he saw: "It was far from a good day. It was thick with fog, rain, drizzle and a southwesterly gale had whipped up a strong swell when we came across the patrol boat, *Otter*. It appeared nothing unusual at first — just a ship on patrol. Then I saw two lifeboats crammed with men drifting away from the craft. I took it to be just exercises but couldn't imagine such in that heavy sea. As I came more closely through the lifting fog, I saw smoke coming from the engine skylights of the boat and then I realized what was wrong."

What the captain saw was a scene of death and the destruction of a Canadian naval vessel. Commanded by Lieutenant Denis S. Mossman, *Otter*, a converted luxury yacht, patrolled the waters near Sambro Light and at the time of her loss was within sight of land. She carried forty-one Royal Canadian Navy seamen, including four officers from Nova Scotia. Although the seas were heavy from a recent storm, it was a routine morning for the crew.

Then at 8:40 a.m., without warning, flames from an unknown origin raced above and below *Otter*'s decks. There was no choice but to abandon ship and heave off the lifeboats and rafts. One lifeboat swamped, throwing its occupants into the icy March seas. Some men clung to a life-raft or "curlyfloat." It had been thrown overboard from *Otter* as men jumped to save themselves from the conflagration. Waves, estimated to be fifteen to twenty feet high, lashed the small craft.

Ten to fifteen minutes after the discovery of the fire, the rescue ship, identified only as a merchantman, pulled alongside and attempted to lower lifeboats. Two were smashed against the side of the ship immediately upon launching. The merchantman pulled as close to the side of *Otter*'s lifeboat as possible considering the high winds and sea, then lowered ladders and ropes over the side. Meanwhile, a Canadian warship appeared and eventually pulled six sailors from the sea. Other seamen from *Otter* bobbed and tossed in the cold sea. Minutes later a third steamer saw the fire and hovered nearby but the only immediate help it could give, and that was determined later to be very valuable, was to manoeuvre into position to serve as a shelter while the other two rescue ships tried to save lives.

Hours later, when all bodies living or dead were pulled from the water and *Otter* was about to take its final plunge, the toll of the sea revealed another sad saga. Nineteen men, a little less than half her crew, had perished. Nova Scotia was heavily represented: nine of those who lived through the battle with fire and sea, and seven who were lost, had connections with Nova Scotia.

Two survivors, Lieutenant Denis Mossman the master, and navigation officer D.A. Snelgrove who lived in Halifax at 274 Oxford Street, were rushed to hospital suffering from shock and exposure. Mossman, also living in Halifax, was born in Chester.

The men who disappeared in the killing waters had clung to the side of a capsized lifeboat, wreckage, or one of *Otter*'s liferafts. Then in the bitter cold of the gale-whipped waters they floated away, chilled to death in their lifebelts.

The skipper of the rescue boat continued his description of the events which followed his initial sighting of the burning *Otter*: "A short distance away, I spotted a partly submerged raft crowded with fifteen or more men and decided to make for it first. But as I steered about, one of the lifeboats — the smaller one — came nearer so I headed for it, planning to pick up its men and save time. As we pulled alongside a huge wave crashed it against the side of my ship and it capsized. I could see men thrown out in all directions.

"We had lowered ladders and ropes all along the sides from our decks, and it was one of these a sailor had grabbed trying to hold the lifeboat fast just before a wave tore it from his hands. Only three men out of more than fifteen in the boat had been able to hold on to the ropes as we pulled them aboard. Many of their shipmates were drowned in that wave that buried their boat, but we saw several figures still in the craft or clinging to it as it came to the surface again. We tried to lower our own lifeboat to pick them out of the sea. One crashed against the posts of its davits in the roll of the waves and was smashed. We turned to the other and it too struck and smashed.

"My crew knew the only alternative. The men down there in the water were too weak to help themselves up the ropes or even fasten them about their bodies. Quickly but coolly, Able Seaman Ptzbylaki, a Polish sailor, tied a rope about his waist and asked a shipmate to lower him over the side. Up to his hips in water he stood in the sinking lifeboat in the mountainous seas, and fastened the navy men, one by one, to another line while those aboard our ship pulled them to safety."

But it was too late for most. Of the six lifted aboard, three were already dead when they reached the deck. Two others, officers of *Otter*, died a short time after. Every man aboard the rescue ship took turns applying artificial respiration and rubbing the bodies of the men with alcohol. "But after two hours," continued the captain, "I saw it was no use — there was nothing we could do."

Meanwhile, the merchant ship had steamed near the second lifeboat with some fifteen men on it including *Otter*'s Lieutenant Mossman. The rescuer, whose name was not revealed, continued his story: "They were in much better shape and were able to climb aboard themselves with little help. Their lifeboat had stood against the sea better than the first one. A short distance away we saw the raft [curlyfloat] and after picking up the second boat we headed for it, but a naval vessel that had appeared on the scene was throwing lines to those men. Although they did everything possible to try and save the men, they brought off only four. The rest on it had died or had washed away."

The rescue ship could see, through the tossing waves, men floating in the water in lifebelts, but there were also empty lifebelts, some thrown from the merchant ship and others from *Otter* that weakened men had not been able to reach. Blankets, wood, and other wreckage lay scattered in the immediate vicinity.

Meanwhile, next to this grisly spectacle of death, the navy craft *Otter* drifted afire and abandoned. As the rescuer remembered: "On one side was the ship [*Otter*] ablaze and by this time from stem to stern. Sometimes we drifted to within a few feet of it realizing it might blow up at any moment. On the other side and around us, were the lifeboats, the raft wreckage and men floating in lifebelts. And for us to fight this terrible nightmare there was a boiling sea. Then came a blast from the yacht, and it turned on end and sank."

Three hours had elapsed. *Otter* was gone. As was revealed later, one of the last acts of *Otter*'s crew before abandonment was to flood the craft's magazine and to ensure the depth charges were disabled.

With the survivors aboard, the rescue ship headed for port. On the way, it met naval craft with medical aid aboard. Doctors climbed onto the freighter, administered further assistance to the navy men, and then transferred the eighteen living and the five dead and took them to shore.

As for the merchant ship that so efficiently rescued many of *Otter*'s men, the story merely reveals it was a drab-toned cargo vessel which had

had several brushes with disaster on the Atlantic since the outbreak of the war. It was the second rescue for the ship within a few years.

Once before it had saved a schooner and its crew of five, after the vessel's mast had broken and left the craft drifting helplessly in mid-Atlantic. The merchant ship captain who described the *Otter* tragedy had fought for his country in World War One as an 18-year-old private. He was captured, held prisoner for two months, and then rescued by the advancing British army. After the war he joined the merchant marine and had been master of the present ship for five years. No doubt he was identified in official government inquiries, but the local newspaper didn't name him because news reports during World War Two were subject to military and government censorship.

One of *Otter's* survivors told how Lieutenant Mossman, a Lunenburg County mariner and a survivor of four previous shipwrecks, had stayed on the ship until the last, ready to go down with it if need be. "Our lifeboat was filled to capacity and we couldn't go back to get him without some of us transferring to the liferaft. I called for volunteers to go and three did. We then went back for the captain. He was standing on the poop deck with the flames beating out from amidships behind him. He got aboard."

The next day, March 29, Mossman spoke, albeit briefly, from his hospital bed. At that time he would give no details of the rescues, the deaths, or the individual acts of heroism, but he did give a blanket compliment to those who had snatched him and his fellows from a killer sea: "They were all simply splendid."

The Nova Scotian seamen who perished that day were: Lieutenant Alan M. Walker, Halifax; Edward T. Wall, Dartmouth; Lionel E. Sturat, Lockeport; Ronald Darrach, Halifax; Chief skipper Andrew F. Parker, Parrsboro; Gerald J. D'Eon, Meteghan River; and Daniel Gillis of Glace Bay and Halifax.

Yarmouth has seen more than its share of wrecks over the years, including the old vessel *City of New York* (above) seen here aground on Chebogue Point, Yarmouth County, with water running over her decks. She was wrecked March 19, 1952. (Photo courtesy Captain Hubert Hall, Shipsearch Marine, Yarmouth)

Netting 323 tons and registered in Honduras, *City of New York* is ashore some time after grounding in March 1952. Salvors comb the wreckage among the surf and rocks of Chebogue Point. (Photo courtesy Bob Brooks)

Chapter 12 (1942-55)
"We hit. Hard!"

One of the last Scaterie Victims

Scaterie Island claimed one of its last schooners on May 5, 1942, when the Lunenburg banker *R.B. Bennett* struck the island's treacherous shoals. By now the era of wooden bankers, which had once sailed out of the traditional fishing ports of Nova Scotia, was drawing to a close.

R.B. Bennett, well known in fishing circles and of a similar design as the famed racing schooner *Bluenose*, netted 100 tons and employed twenty-six Nova Scotian fishermen. Her owners, W.C. Smith and Company, put the capable Captain Albert Crouse in charge of the 12-year-old Lunenburg-built vessel.

It was 3:30 p.m. in dense fog. *R.B. Bennett* was headed for Louisbourg for bait when she stranded at Point Howe. When it became obvious to Crouse that his schooner was beyond salvage, he ordered his crew into the dories. All personal belongings and extra clothes were left behind. After a six-hour row in thick fog, they reached land near Louisbourg. Wet and cold, *R.B. Bennett*'s crew was given warm clothes and shelter before they were taken to North Sydney. From there on May 6, the crew caught the express train for Halifax en route to Lunenburg.

Bastian (left) ended her days at White Point. Clement's of Burgeo, Newfoundland, owned the Danish tern schooner *Bastian*, commanded by Captain Arch Matthews, but lost her in November 1940 at White Point near Canso, Cape Breton. Matthews went on to captain *Beatrice Beck* — the schooner disappeared three years later with Matthews and his Burgeo shipmates, Elias Anderson, who had fought in France in The Great War, and Leonard Anderson, no relation to Elias.

Tragedy at White Point, six miles from Canso

In the fall of 1943 *Wally G*, a 60-ton schooner, set sail from Halifax en route to the Magdalen Islands in the Gulf of St. Lawrence. Aboard was a cargo of mostly food and gasoline loaded at Halifax. Captain Joseph "Joe" Emberley took the short route through the Strait of Canso instead of travelling around the tip of Nova Scotia.

Wally G was built in 1910 at Grand Bank, Newfoundland, for Spencer's at nearby Fortune. In time this 78-foot long schooner was sold to various owners including Samuel Harris of Grand Bank. Now on October 7, 1943, in the last hours of her long career, she coasted Nova Scotia's shores delivering cargo to various ports while under charter to A. Burke and Company, Halifax.

She carried four crewmen. Captain Emberley, aged 50, was born at English Harbour East, had gone to sea at a young age and then settled in Nova Scotia. He lived at 1 Poplar Grove, Halifax. Emberley had been shipwrecked twice before. Twelve years previously when master of *Katherine M*, he survived her burning and he was also shipwrecked on a freighter in the Gulf of St. Lawrence. Joe Emberley had one arm, yet was a skilled seaman and veteran captain who certainly didn't let a physical disability stand in his way.

Also aboard *Wally G* was William Emberley, the captain's nephew, aged 17 and residing on Gannon Road, North Sydney. The lad had wanted to sail with his uncle and Captain Emberley agreed. The other two were Alan MacDonald, 50, of Ochterloney Street, Dartmouth, who owned the little coaster, and cook Albert Trenholm, 63, of 31 Birmingham Street, Halifax.

About 5:30 a.m., the captain saw trouble ahead — white breakers glistening along the blackness where sea and sky meet. There was a stiff wind blowing; *Wally G*, although equipped with a small engine, had a main sail up while navigating through Chedabucto Bay. Ploughing along in a good breeze the little coaster piled onto a reel off White Point with a tremendous force.

Immediately *Wally G* pounded upon the rocks and, with the roiling combers around her, began to break up. Emberley recalled: "I was just coming up on deck from below where I had gone to get a warm up, when I heard the crew talking about having seen land. Then suddenly I saw the breakers. I shouted to the engineer to start the engine, for we were under sail at the time and I thought we might be able to pull her away. Just before I reached the engine room, we hit. Hard!"

After he called to the engineer, Captain Emberley ran to the wheel to assist Albert Trenholm who was having his turn at the helm. As Emberley reached his side, *Wally G* ground to a halt on the shoals. In a matter of minutes, she took several heavy blows and fell to pieces. The spars fell onto the decks and soon the choppy water was full of debris and tossing wreckage.

Alan MacDonald jumped into the sea to try to reach the rocks, but he disappeared in the cold water. Billy Emberley, the captain's nephew, was washed away by one of the many waves that crashed over her deck. He managed to grab the grounded stern section and stayed there for quite some time. Trenholm was also washed off the shattered boat and he too disappeared from the captain's sight.

With only seconds to decide, Joseph Emberley jumped clear of the sinking schooner and got out into the heaving wreckage, trying to find a piece to hold on to. He reached a large piece of deck planking. The captain knew his young nephew was still holding on at the stern and it was

A cutwater schooner, *Wally G* (above) is tied on and awaiting produce at Montague, PEI. In the background are Poole & Thompson Ltd. (left) and Johnstone's Flour and Feed (right). At the time the photograph was taken *Wally G* was commanded by Newell Piercey of Fortune, Newfoundland. (Photo courtesy Mrs. Janie Piercey)

his intention to push this makeshift liferaft near the stern section. Wind and sea prevented him from manoeuvring near, but he called to Billy to let go of the wreckage and swim to him. The young man was either too weak or too frightened to let go. Eventually he lost his hold and slipped into the sea. Joe Emberley recalled the sad moment: "I kept telling him to swim for the raft but he wouldn't. He clung to the stern. Sometimes he would give one or the other arm a rest when he managed to throw a leg up over the stern. The sea was sweeping over him and what remained of the ship. Then he called out, 'I can't hold on any longer, Uncle Joe,' and went down."

Although despondent at his nephew's death, who had drowned before his eyes, and by the loss of two other shipmates the captain soon regained his determination to stay alive. Despite having only one arm, Emberley had incredible determination and strength. After a struggle he managed to get the section of planking through the snarl of tossing wreckage and he began to drift to sea. For eight or nine hours he had stayed near the rock and stern section of *Wally G*.

When Emberley saw a wave about to break on the raft, which measured about six by seven feet, he grabbed a ringbolt attached to the decking and clung on for his life. As the waves pounded around him, he tried to hold on with his one arm and scan the horizon in every direction for a sign of a ship. He knew he was near the much travelled Gut of Canso and the possibility of another vessel passing by was great.

About four or five p.m., nearly twelve hours after the wreck, he saw a steamer. He could see it had a course which would take the ship close to him; thus he was determined to signal. In the gathering dusk, he knew it was his last chance. Taking off his wet coat, he raised himself to a semi-standing position on the tossing raft and waved the coat over his head.

Fortunately, although it was now at the close of day, someone on the bridge of the steamer saw the figure and reported to the captain — a man adrift! While the steamer stood by, a boat was lowered and soon helpful hands had Joseph Emberley safely aboard the steamer. To Emberley's surprise one of the men aboard the steamer was Lee Hartigan of Rencontre East, Newfoundland, a town not far from Emberley's home in English Harbour East. Hartigan was a boyhood friend. Emberley had not seen Hartigan for many years but recognized him as soon as he stepped aboard the steamer, which in itself is a remarkable story of coincidence. Aboard the steamer, Captain Emberley told the sad tale of the loss of three crewmates and the wreck of *Wally G.*

He was taken to Halifax. From his hospital bed Emberley related the loss of the schooner to a newspaper reporter and he had the sad duty of informing loved ones of the death of three men. Captain Joseph Emberley, with one arm, had an extraordinary story of survival — one man against the sea in a twelve-hour struggle to stay alive.

Ethel M. Petite on Sister's Shoal

On February 5, 1948, *Ethel M. Petite* headed for Halifax harbour loaded with cod. At three a.m. she piled onto the Sister's Shoal or Ledge, a reef three miles off Chebucto Head, near Halifax. Forced into dories in temperatures that dipped well below freezing, the twenty-eight man crew, under the direction of Captain Arch Evans of English Harbour West, Newfoundland, rowed toward the mainland.

Most men had been sleeping when the schooner hit the rocks, and had barely enough time to haul on their clothes and gather a few belongings before abandoning ship. In the bitter cold and dark, several dories went in different directions. Twelve men in four dories were picked up by the Halifax harbour pilot boat; the other sixteen men in four dories rowed to Ketch Harbour, not far from Halifax.

When word of the grounding reached Halifax, the RCMP cutter *Irvine* and the navy tug *Glenbrook* went to the scene, but by then the schooner was partly submerged and beyond salvage. Her catch of 100,000 pounds of fish, valued at $5,000, was lost to the sea.

Marshall Frank at Framboise Cove

Marshall Frank was one of several banking schooners owned or managed by James M. Petite of Halifax. Her crew of twenty-five, including Captain Abe Myles, were all from Newfoundland. On February 17, 1949, the 144-ton schooner grounded on Marie Joseph Shoals, twenty-two miles south of Sydney.

When the snow and sleet struck at four p.m., some of the dorymen were still at their trawls. When all men and dories were aboard, *Marshall Frank* left the banks for Halifax to wait out the impending storm. Eleven hours later, while en route to Halifax, a grinding jar told Captain Myles his schooner was aground.

With *Marshall Frank* heeled over in shallow water, seven- and eight-foot waves forced the men to hold on to anything they could grip. Although within sight of land, Myles knew he and his men had to get in the dories and row out to sea to survive dangerous rocks and shoals near shore. To attempt beaching a dory through high breakers on unfamiliar shores could be disastrous to all.

Twenty men boarded five dories and rowed out to sea, away from the shoal of rock and the stranded schooner. The sixth dory to leave had five men — Leo and Conrad Blagdon of Boxey, Garfield Greene and Norman Ball of Rencontre West, and John Sam Blagdon of Coomb's Cove — who may have had difficulty getting away from *Marshall Frank*. Sometime between four a.m. and daybreak on the morning of February 16, all five drowned as they attempted to get the dory away from the wrecked schooner.

Her back broken, *Marshall Frank* lies near the shore at Framboise Cove. (Photo courtesy Randell Pope)

A little after daylight, when the wind changed and the remaining survivors could see land, they rowed toward Framboise Cove. One dory landed by the old wharf near an abandoned lobster factory, two miles south of the wreck. Four other dories breached the enormous breakers; one overturned, throwing the occupants into the water, but all made it safely to shore. The men walked inland to some homes near Marie Joseph. With their clothes dried and strength regained, the crew went back to the beach near the stranded *Marshall Frank* to search for their missing friends and to salvage any belongings from the wreck.

That same day, the bodies of Leo Blagdon and Garfield Greene were found near the wreck and the other three were located later. *Marshall Frank* had driven in over the shoal to within a few feet of the shore.

Returned to die at Whitehead

A pilot boat with twenty years service in Halifax returned to die on Nova Scotian shores. *Nauphila*, a 95-foot pilot boat servicing Halifax harbour from 1926 until 1946, was sold to John King of Fortune, Newfoundland, and had been used in the Newfoundland–Nova Scotia coastal run for two years.

Nauphila had left Fortune bound for Halifax Friday, December 10, but met a typical winter northeasterly gale. She lay to until Sunday before continuing her slow progress toward Nova Scotia.

On Tuesday night in a blinding snowstorm, while heavy seas pounded *Nauphila*, the helmsman mistook the Whitehead light for Scaterie light. When the freighter struck the rocks, she began to break up quickly. The crew — Captain George "Nick" Collier, owner John King, seaman Chris Hebditch, all of Fortune, Maxwell Collins of Lamaline, and John H. Ayres of Point Crew — tried to launch a dory but it was swept away. Fortunately there was a second one aboard. Captain Collier was injured and had to be thrown into the dory from *Nauphila*'s deck when waves prevented him from being lowered over the side.

Waves swept the fragile craft ashore and onto an unfamiliar coast. In the darkness and against the lee of a cliff they crouched on a rocky beach, huddled against the wind and blizzard. Finally the tired men found an abandoned fisherman's shack and built a fire. Twenty-seven hours after they had jumped from the wrecked *Nauphila*, the storm abated and seas on that lonely, isolated beach finally subsided. On Wednesday morning, December 15, they launched their dory and eventually Nauphila's five exhausted seaman rowed the ten miles into the small anchorage of Whitehead, Guysborough County.

Autauga at Cape St. Lawrence

In early September 1951, *Autauga*, crewed by Newfoundland men, was en route to North Sydney from Georgetown, PEI, with products from the island — hay, cheese and 300 logs to be used in wharf construction in Newfoundland. Before daylight on Saturday morning, September 8, she crashed ashore and sank on Cape Breton's western coast.

Captain Pius Augot believed his compass was out and that had caused the 26-year-old *Autauga* to hit the rocks at the base of a steep cliff, about seven miles west of Cape St. Lawrence. Her crew — including the captain's 8-year-old son, engineer Reg Augot (the captain's brother), cook Jesse Bishop, mate John Stone, Phil Augot, George Stone, and Jack Stone — all boarded an open dory. In two hours they found a sheltered cove on the rocky coast where the dory could be safely beached.

Kent Sweeney (above) was blown ashore in Yarmouth harbour by Hurricane Edna in September 1954. (Photo courtesy Captain Hubert Hall, Shipsearch Marine, Yarmouth)

Burning of Lunenburg schooner *Bessemer*

By the 1950s, technological advances in long-distance communication, radar, sonar and directional finding devices had made sea voyages and shipping much safer. Accidents on the ocean were reduced, but occasionally collisions, fog, harsh weather, and the age-old nemesis fire, claimed their share of vessels.

On July 31, 1953, the Lunenburg schooner *Bessemer* was fishing about forty miles southeast of Halifax. About 2:30 a.m. Captain Garfield Anstey was pulled from his bunk by the second engineer, one of three men who were awake when fire broke out in the engine room.

The 158-ton *Bessemer*, based out of Lunenburg, carried twenty-one crewmen: six Nova Scotians and fifteen Newfoundlanders. Jointly owned by James M. Petite of Halifax and Captain Anstey, *Bessemer* was fully insured.

The engineers discovered smoke coming from the engine room; one ran to inform the captain and another ran to the forecastle to rouse the eighteen sleeping there. One crewman, William Dominaux of Hare Harbour, Newfoundland, was overcome by fumes while in his bunk, but his mates pulled him to safety. Captain Anstey twice tried to raise the marine

Bessemer (above at Lunenburg), built in 1928 by Smith & Rhuland, measured 120 feet long with a 27-foot beam. The sails of a dory dry on her deck. On July 31, 1953, *Bessemer* was destroyed by fire. (Photo courtesy C.F. McBride and Captain Hubert Hall, Shipsearch Marine, Yarmouth)

radio station at Halifax but to no avail. The radio went dead and Anstey, the last man aboard, jumped into one of the seven dories the crew had launched. It was three o'clock, a half hour after the shout of "Fire! Fire!" first sounded.

Anstey recalled: "The after deck was full of smoke. You couldn't see anything. Men were going everywhere, running for their lives. I gathered some food and water for when we took to the dories. We knew she would go down because she was gradually settling in the water. The fuel tanks kept exploding and an air tank was blown through the side of the ship."

The captain had no idea how the fire started, but did state it was his first shipwreck in twenty-five years at sea. At 9:45 in the morning they were still within sight of *Bessemer* and watched her go down. The seven dories drifted for seventeen hours before the men were picked up by the schooner *L.A. Dunton*. They were then transferred to *Muriel Isabel*, also owned by James Petite, Anstey's business partner.

On May 5, 1955, another coastal vessel was wrecked. The 130-ton *Joan Garland*, en route from Montague, Prince Edward Island, to Newfoundland, grounded at White Point, Nova Scotia. She became a total loss, though Captain George White and his crew escaped unscathed.

When *Dorothy P. Sarty* (above at Digby) sank late in the evening of June 12, 1954, her crew took to the lifeboat, refused a pickup and rowed to Nova Scotia's coast. Owned in Newfoundland, the 85-ton coaster sprang a leak twenty-four hours after leaving North Sydney. When Captain Frank Poole saw there was no way to stop the inflow of water he ordered his men over the side. Her crew — engineer Nauss Piercey, aged 37; cook Vince Savoury, 40; William Poole, 60; Philip Keating, 28; and Clyde Poole, 31, all residents of Belleoram — rowed twenty-five miles back to Lingan, Nova Scotia. The *Sarty* sank carrying 150 tons of Sydney coal destined for Badger's Quay, Newfoundland. (Photo Courtesy C.F. McBride and Captain Hubert Hall, Ship-search Marine, Yarmouth)

Miss Glenburnie

Sam Pardy and his crew spent seven hours in a dory with no belongings and only a compass to guide them after they were rammed by an unknown ship.

The 84-ton *Miss Glenburnie*, owned by J.B. Patten of Grand Bank, left Halifax and headed for home on May 25, 1955, when, about twenty-five miles east of Halifax, a large vessel appeared out of dense fog, struck the schooner and steamed on without stopping. Pardy freed the dory from the sinking *Glenburnie* and steered a course for land before he and his crew were picked up by *Josephine K*.

Meanwhile *Sun Prince*, inbound to Halifax from Montreal, had stopped engines after the collision, listened for signs of distress but heard nothing. Officials from Saguenay Terminals, owners of the *Sun Prince*, later confirmed the accident.

The 70-ton *Beatrice and Grace*, (above at Bay L'Argent, where she was once owned by Frank Bond) was built to fish the Grand Banks, but at the end of her career plied the coastal trade. On September 2, 1955, she loaded coal at North Sydney and left for Lamaline, Newfoundland, but sank four hours out of port. Engineer Joseph Myles noticed water trickling in around the propeller shaft and notified Captain Austin Myles. When all efforts to stop the severe leaking failed, Myles radioed for help. The Glace Bay vessel *Annie Margaret* hove into sight and Captain Myles gave orders to abandon ship. (Photo courtesy Alex Hardy)

Chapter 13 (1956-67)
The sea takes four

Heroism at sea takes many forms. But none is so memorable as that of one man who, among his shipmates, volunteers himself and alone tries to rescue all. He swims from a wreck through high waves, climbs over rock and kelp-strewn boulders in freezing temperatures. At the moment he, encumbered by clothes and a rope tied around his waist, is about to gain land, a wave smashes him against the rocks and he suffers a crippling injury.

Heroism at Portuguese Cove

The date is January 6, 1956; the wrecked vessel *Cape Agulhas* is grounded at Portuguese Cove, and twenty men face certain death. The details of events leading up to the wreck are given through the words of *Cape Agulhas*' captain, Jack Lilly of Halifax: "*Cape Agulhas* sank in fifty feet of water about ten minutes after she grounded in the dense fog and black of the night just before dawn. We must have come in too far. It was very unexpected when we struck. I've come in here many times, but there was fog and the seas were very, very heavy."

The 150-foot steam trawler, "flying blind" according to Lilly, with her sounding equipment and radar out of order, struck and grounded at Portuguese Cove near the mouth of Halifax harbour. With navigating

Cape Agulhas carried 120,000 pounds of fish for Halifax's National Sea fish processing company when she grounded and sank at Portuguese Cove on January 6, 1956. (Photo courtesy Alex Hardy)

equipment useless for several hours, *Cape Agulhas* had crept along the coast at three knots before striking the reef, tearing a gaping hole in her hull. "It all happened so fast we hardly had time to think," concluded Lilly.

But someone had to act fast to save the lives of twenty men and this is where the physical strength and mental toughness of Ernest Thornhill reached heroic proportions. Ernest Thornhill was born in the seaside town of Fortune, Newfoundland, in 1925 and first went to sea at age fourteen. By 1956 he had already left home and with his wife, five sons and one daughter lived in West Dover, Nova Scotia. There he was near his work on the National Sea Products trawlers.

Built in Selby, England in 1919, the 324-ton *Cape Agulhas* was originally named *John W. Johnson*. In 1937 she operated under the Newfoundland government's Ministry of Fisheries as a research/patrol vessel and later fished for the Belleoram Trawling Company. By the 1950s she was based out of Halifax.

Thornhill was mate on *Cape Agulhas* when an early January storm forced the trawler to leave the Grand Banks and, on January 6, to seek shelter in Halifax.

When all hope of saving *Cape Agulhas* was given up, it seemed that the chance of saving the lives of the crew members of the vessel was very near hopeless as well. It was then that Ernest Thornhill volunteered to risk his life in an attempt to get to shore with a line.

After fastening a line around his waist, he bade his pals good-bye and plunged into the freezing, pounding surf in a "do or die" attempt to swim to shore. This heroic seaman fought the surf and the breakers and after a terrific battle with the hostile elements, he reached the shore with a fractured leg. In addition he had severe gashes in his arms and back from the pounding he received while swimming the 200 feet or more to land. However, he managed to fasten the line around a big boulder and by means of the line the rest of the crewmen made their way through the surf and jagged rocks to the shore.

After receiving some welcome attention from the people of the cove, Thornhill spent ten days in Camp Hill Hospital and for three months was confined to his home. On April 6, exactly three months after the dramatic rescue, Ernest Thornhill reported back to work as bosun with National Sea on *Cape Brier*. He was later asked, "Did you ever think of quitting the sea?" Thornhill replied, "No, it's the only thing I know."

For his bravery Ernest Thornhill was awarded both the Silver Medal of the Royal Canadian Humane Society and the coveted George Medal, the top civilian award for courage given by the United Kingdom. Other tributes flowed in as well: a gold watch presented by Mayor Kitz on behalf of the city of Halifax, a wristwatch presented by broadcasting station CJCH, and a cheque from National Sea Products.

Residents of Portuguese Cove gave immediate help to the shipwrecked crew of *Cape Agulhas*, and many people there still remember and marvel at Thornhill's selfless deed. His shipmates on *Cape Agulhas*, who afterwards were scattered on other vessels of dragger fleets, always claimed that Thornhill was one who gallantly offered his life so they could live.

But the final chapter for Thornhill came dramatically some six years later, when, at the age of 37, he was a crewman on the trawler *Red Diamond III* operated by Booth Fisheries Canada of Petit-de-Grat. While at sea in a storm he was struck and knocked down by a warp (steel cable) which had broken loose from a deck roller. He received compound leg fractures and internal injuries. At the time *Red Diamond* was 250 miles south of Cape Race and out of helicopter range. Thornhill was transferred to the Greek liner *Queen Frederica*, which answered the distress call. While on the liner bound for Halifax, he had a leg amputated but passed away in a Halifax hospital from his injuries. The date was January 25, 1962.

Sambro swordfisher, *Angela B. Mills*

By the 1950s the swordfishing industry of Nova Scotia was a lucrative trade. But pursuing an elusive fish on the broad expanses of the Atlantic is fraught with danger. The whereabouts of an age-old enemy, the August or September Gales, now known to be the tail end of seasonal hurricanes, could now be predicted more accurately.

On Saturday night, August 18, 1956, the crew of the swordfishing boat *Angela B. Mills* listened to radio reports of Hurricane Betsy as the windstorm romped northward along the eastern coastline. The crew felt assured it was too far away to threaten the 85-foot vessel and they turned in for the night. Little did they know at that point, they would battle angry seas and high winds not in the relative comfort of an enclosed fishing craft but in a makeshift cockleshell exposed to all nature's elements.

In her August trip on the Grand Banks the 39-ton *Angela B. Mills*, owned by Harold Henneberry and Charles Marryatt, had taken sixty-two large swordfish in four days, a substantial catch representing a good pay cheque for her crew. All crewmen, except one, were from the Sambro district, near Halifax: Captain Harold Henneberry, aged 41; Charles Burke, Louisbourg; Roy Marryatt, Halifax; Charles Marryatt; Herbert Marryatt, Long Cove; Melvin Gray; and Keith Gray.

In the night, one of the crew heard a loud snap or crack. He went on deck to determine the cause and seeing nothing, returned to his bunk. A little later one of the other men went down to the hold to look around and came back with an alarm, "Water rising fast!"

Captain Henneberry pointed out: "Water in the boat came up that quick, but there was no way of knowing what happened to *Angela B. Mills*. We think a plank must have sprung off the bottom. Winds were about twenty-five knots. It wasn't a sea that hurt that boat. We had more wind when we were in the dories."

Abandon ship! Two dreaded words made all the more frightening when a crew has to board a small dory in the middle of the Atlantic with little food or water. Before the men had time to properly prepare the dories, the lights on *Angela B.* went out. As Henneberry recalled: "We had quite a bit of food in the first dory but the stern of the boat came down on her and smashed her and we lost all that. We had no lights and groped around the sinking craft to find more food. Finally we rounded up twenty-three cans of spaghetti soup and some orange juice and a gallon of water. We never had enough food for one man, but we put water in the soup and tried to keep going."

With barely enough food for one person, the seven stepped into two or three small boats in the treacherous seas off southern Newfoundland. In the best of times the open seas are often choppy and, with any amount of wind, heavy seas can break across larger ships. Reports of a pending hurricane were fresh in their minds as they tied the dories together, put rubber tires between them to keep from smashing each other, and attempted to row in the general direction of land.

On Wednesday an airplane located the first sign of wreckage of *Angela B. Mills*, but saw no sign of a lifeboat or dory. By now the men had been adrift for three-and-a-half days and were quite a distance from where their boat went down. When no word had been received from the vessel or the men, relatives in Nova Scotia grew anxious. By Thursday and Friday, the unspeakable questions surfaced: ashore, wrecked, lost at sea?

By the third night out the weary men couldn't row. Winds had picked up to thirty knots an hour and several times the makeshift flotilla nearly capsized. Every wave threatened death during those days and nights. Not knowing how long their meagre food supply would have to last, it was carefully rationed. A gun and a few bullets had been stashed aboard one of the dories. When a seabird came within range, they shot at it but rough seas spoiled their aim and bullets were wasted. They did manage to kill one bird. One of the crew later said the raw bird was "not bad when you have to eat it."

The captain continued his story: "The second or third night we were out, we saw a plane three or four miles away. We thought it might have ben searching for us but it didn't see us. [I] have been fishing since about twelve years old but, like the rest of the crew, I had never been shipwrecked. Some of us got only about two hours sleep during the entire time we were in the boats and were so exhausted we couldn't sleep when we got ashore."

It was Sunday, August 26, and the crew of *Angela B. Mills* had rowed and drifted for seven-and-a-half days. They were about three miles off Trepassey, near Newfoundland's eastern tip, when fishermen Allan and Lyle Sutton and John Penney found them and towed the dories ashore.

Each man had lost about eighteen pounds and all were exhausted from lack of sleep and proper food. They were taken to St. John's and lodged in the Red Cross hostel. On Monday night Henneberry, Herbert and Roy Marryatt, and Keith Gray took the Trans Canada Airlines flight home to happy relatives, while the remaining three followed soon after.

Men who follow the sea often face extreme odds and arduous physical privations, but in the end find a grim humour to it all. As Henneberry said the day after rescue, "We're not too spruce yet. Shaky on our legs. I suppose I aged about ten years, so right now I'm about 51 years old."

Joyce and Doreen, lost at Louisbourg

The 48-ton *Joyce and Doreen*, powered by a 150-horsepower Caterpillar engine and equipped for halibut fishing, was owned by Captain Arch Evans of Newfoundland.

On August 13, 1957, Evans and his crew — cook John Fizzard, Montford Piercey, Philip Fizzard, Abe George Hillier, all of Grand Bank, Allen Keeping from English Harbour West, and Amos Poole of Belleoram — fished on Sable Island Bank. On the horizon they could see the low silouette of the island, but kept their distance from the treacherous sand bars off its shores.

They had done well with fishing that summer. *Joyce and Doreen* was loaded with around 15,000 pounds of halibut. Although Evans and his crew sought mostly halibut, swordfish was a valuable species bringing good prices in Nova Scotian ports. They had harpooned twelve swordfish, each averaging about a thousand pounds and these were iced away in the holds. *Joyce and Doreen* made for Louisbourg to discharge her profitable catch.

When the twelve o'clock sounding was made that night, *Joyce and Doreen* was on course. She was not equipped with radar, thus the helmsman could not see land or danger ahead. Three hours later, the vessel struck land about one-and-a-half miles from Louisbourg harbour. The noise and jolt awakened the five crewmen sleeping below, but they lost no time jumping into their clothes and boots. By the time they and Captain Evans, who had been asleep in the wheelhouse cabin, reached the deck the small dory was already in the water with one man aboard. *Joyce and*

Doreen struck side on, a little offshore, on an underwater ledge and listed on her starboard side.

Within a few minutes the second and larger dory was launched, or "hove off," on the port side and the remaining crew clambered aboard. To distribute the numbers, two men transferred to the smaller dory. Although some men managed to grab their suitcases, most lost clothes and personal belongings. Since the crew was in no immediate danger, they waited near the wreck until daylight, when they could better see their location and could make their way to Louisbourg. About an hour later, the lights of the stranded vessel attracted a Louisbourg fisherman who was out tending his gear. In the mutual agreement of help on the sea, the man used his skiff to tow the dories into Louisbourg.

Later that day Captain Evans engaged two longliners to attach tow lines to *Joyce and Doreen*, but she refused to budge — the vessel and cargo became a total loss and the crew had to find a ride to North Sydney. There, two Grand Bank schooners were in port: *Freda M*, skippered by Captain George Follett, and Captain Ben Snook's *Nina W. Corkum*. The crew stayed aboard *Freda M* for a night or two, then took the gulf ferry to Port aux Basques and returned home by train to Goobies where transportation to Grand Bank awaited them.

For Philip Fizzard, it was his second shipwreck: he had been a crewman on *Ethel M. Petite*, which wrecked in 1948. In 1959 when the side trawler *Blue Wave* went down, he was one of the crew who was lost.

Near a graveyard of wrecks at Bay St. Lawrence

At Bay St. Lawrence, a place where the ribs and broken skeletons of other shipwrecked schooners stuck out of the water, the 246-ton *Bermuda Clipper* also left her bones. En route from Prince Edward Island to North Sydney to load coal, the coastal schooner ran into a reef near this tiny community near the tip of Cape Breton Island. By October 10, 1960, fishermen reported that the *Bermuda Clipper* was fast going to pieces. By then, she had already been stripped of salvageable equipment and her stern and keel posts had been knocked out by heavy wave action. Captain Tom Snook of Grand Bank and his crew, having tried unsuccessfully to have *Bermuda Clipper* pulled free, had already left for their Newfoundland homes.

Sydney Naval Base "Good to be here"

"I'm still trying to figure out what made the vessel go down. It all happened so fast. But it's good to be here in Sydney," said Captain Garfield Anstey, just after he and his crew landed at Point Edward Naval Base.

Anstey told the story of the 93-foot *Muriel Isabel* which sank Thursday, October 20, 1960, about ninety miles east of Cape Breton. The crew had finished dinner around eleven a.m. Thursday, when the cook, Reuben Stoodley, went below to check the level of fresh water in the tank. He saw more than he expected — sea water was rising rapidly in the hold. Captain Anstey rushed below and tried to start the four water pumps, only to discover two were under water and useless.

Anstey recalled: "When I noticed this [the malfunctioning pumps and the water gaining in the hold], I knew *Muriel Isabel* was gone. I sent a distress signal and heard the fishing vessel *Red Diamond II* was in the area. I wasn't afraid because I knew she would come to our assistance. When the water started pouring in we didn't feel too good. We were glad to see the *Red Diamond II* and we were picked up at 1:30 p.m. On the way in we were transferred to the US coastal cutter *Barataria* which landed us near Sydney."

Muriel Isabel, en route to North Sydney with 15,000 pounds of fish, carried nine crewmen: Captain Anstey and his son Alvin, aged 24; William Foote, 38; Charles Foote, 43, all residents of Halifax; Gerry Hackett, 43, and Raymond Bartlett, 41, lived in Lunenburg; Max Fiander, 42, of Back Point; and John Fudge, 56, and cook Stoodley, aged 31, lived in Newfoundland. Captain Anstey, part owner of the vessel, figured the value of the loss was $55,000.

It was not the first time he had been forced to abandon a vessel at sea. "I recall," he said, "in 1953 when the *Bessemer* caught fire and sank about fifty miles off Halifax. I was on that vessel at the time. The *Muriel Isabel* was equipped with three small dories, but I'm mighty glad we didn't have to use them!"

Chief Engineer Foote, like the rest of the crew, could not understand how the *Muriel Isabel* sprang a leak so quickly. For Foote, it was the second time in three years he was forced to escape from a sinking vessel. He was on *Joan Ellamae* when she went down May 2, 1957.

Captain Anstey voiced his opinion on what it might have been like in an open dory on a choppy ocean: "The *Barataria* was rocking when en route here due to heavy seas. You can well imagine what it would have been like if we were forced to take to the dories. If a large coastal vessel like her rocked, what would a dory have done in open seas? Yes, we're glad to be here at the naval yard today. But I will go back to sea when we get a new boat."

Mary Sweeney (above) was blown ashore in Yarmouth harbour in December 1962. (Photo courtesy Captain Hubert Hall, Shipsearch Marine, Yarmouth)

Nova Scotian seas — *Maureen and Michael, Cape Bonnie, Iceland II, Polly and Robbie*

For several days in late February 1967, air-sea search and rescue units — four RCAF Argus aircraft, two Albatross planes, and two Neptune patrol planes of the United States Air Force — scoured the seas off Newfoundland and Nova Scotia and eventually located what they thought was debris of the missing ship *Polly and Robbie*. But the wreckage probably belonged to *Maureen and Michael*, a schooner which went down off St. Pierre after her crew had been rescued by the US Coast Guard.

The US Coast Guard cutter *Castle Rock* rescued *Maureen and Michael*'s crew: Captain Max Fiander, of Halifax, formerly of English Harbour West, Newfoundland; Isaac and Seward Bartlett of Coomb's Cove, and later residents of Grand Bank; William Hardiman and William

The Nova Scotian fishing vessel *Maureen and Michael* is shown sinking stern first in the cold seas off Newfoundland. She was caught in a storm on February 21-23, 1967, which claimed three ships and their crewmen: *Polly and Robbie, Iceland II* and *Cape Bonnie*. Two US Coast Guard personnel from *Castle Rock* had to don wetsuits and take a rubber raft to the *Maureen and Michael* to ensure the safety of all. Rescuer Pettek said: "The stern was going down as we got there. One guy jumped aboard the raft . . . the raft drifted away and we had to pull it back to get the other man. We were only about fifty yards away in the raft when the ship sank." (Photo of picture in Motel Mortier, Marystown, Newfoundland)

Dominaux, Bay L'Argent; John Ben Strowbridge, Jersey Harbour; John Tom Tibbo of Harbour Breton, who resided in Liscomb, Nova Scotia; and Conrad Mills of Louisbourg.

The Lockeport vessel *Polly and Robbie*, an 85-ton longliner owned by Captain Edwin Brewer, which had steamed to help *Maureen and Michael* was not so fortunate. The 48-ton *Polly and Robbie*, only two years old, went down with all of her seven men: Captain Brewer, aged 39, and his brother Randall, 50, both born in Epworth, Newfoundland but residing in Lockeport; Isaac Wells, 59, of Grand Bank, who in 1965 had been the cook on the halibut fishing vessel *Marjorie and Dorothy* and had recently signed on *Polly and Robbie*; the other four crewmen were from Nova Scotia — James White, 25, Lockeport; brothers Currie, 21, and Harold Harnish, 18; and Reid Jollimore of Mill Cove.

According to the last transmitted message from *Polly and Robbie*, when she was about 100 miles south of Cape Race, a sea (estimated that night to be 40-foot waves) hit her which probably ripped off the cabin and stove in the sides. Winds, measured by Newfoundland weather stations to be in excess of 100 miles an hour, pushed up seas so mountainous that no ship of any size could turn broadside to them and hope to survive. After six days of search and rescue efforts, searchers found the side of a deck house with an attached life preserver bearing the name *Polly and Robbie*, a dory and other debris.

The week of sea disasters began on Tuesday morning, February 21, when *Cape Bonnie*, a trawler racing to make Halifax harbour in the storm, grounded on a ledge off Woody Island one mile from the shore of Pennant Bay. In the raging storm, *Cape Bonnie* was off course and was carried into the waters near Sambro ledges, one of the most treacherous coastlines on the Atlantic coast located twelve miles west of Halifax harbour. The wreck scene was about ten miles west of where the Panamanian freighter *Tegean* ran aground on a reef the previous November 28, with no loss of life.

According to investigators, the crew may have believed they had struck the dreaded Sister's Ledge and left the trawler quickly in lifeboats. All were lost. Built in Britain in 1952, *Cape Bonnie* carried direction-finding, echo-sounding, and radio-telephone equipment as well as radar, but possibly the ship's radar failed.

Throughout the four- or five-day storm, *Cape Bonnie*, a 400-ton trawler laden with 70,000 pounds of fish for National Sea Products of Halifax, was still partly afloat, but searchers and rescue units were unable to reach the wreck. Sixteen of her crew (some with ages recorded) were: Captain Hickey aged 42; Bernard Joseph Cashen, 23; Clement Andrew Thompson, 20; Leo Charles LeBlanc, 39; Kenneth William Spidell, 23; John Hector Newcombe, 21, all from Halifax; bosun William Wilneff, 20, and chief engineer Andrew Malcolm of Dartmouth; Murray Garfield Turner, 28, Truro; mate Bernard Hebditch, St. Pierre-Miquelon; Howard Joseph Gastie, West Bay Centre, Newfoundland; Larry Gainsford, Summerville, NS; Moyle Baxter Covey, 40, Indian Harbour, NS; Lloyd Banford Dunphy, 20, Wellington Station, NS; William Brushette, 60; and Richard Landry, 20.

Two views of *Cape Bonnie*, grounded near Pennant Bay, Nova Scotia, on February 21, 1967. Fog, snow, and freezing spray cut visibility to a few feet as *Cape Bonnie* passed three navigational buoys normally visible on radar screens. With the radar out, she had wandered several miles off course into some of the most treacherous waters on the Atlantic coast. (Photos courtesy Jack Keeping)

Captain Gerald Bartlett of *Kathleen B*, a fishing vessel which recovered six bodies from the sea, reported them as wearing lifejackets, which led him to believe the trawler's two lifeboats upset. "Once in the water," Bartlett said, "the men couldn't survive. The water is too cold." Other *Cape Bonnie*'s victims were found along the shoreline. From the clothes they wore, investigators concluded the vessel was abandoned soon after it grounded.

But *Cape Bonnie* was not the last victim of that February storm. Throughout the blizzard, authorities on shore knew another ship — the 91-foot stern trawler *Iceland II* — was in difficulty off Cape Breton.

The silence from the vessel was ominous. Then, on Saturday, February 26, 17-year-old Brian MacKay, out walking on the beach near his home at Fourchu, saw the wrecked trawler, a derelict near the shore. Her fate was similar to that of *Cape Bonnie*. Apparently Iceland II was trying to make Louisbourg in the storm and grounded at high speed, probably with her crew not knowing she was off course. No radio calls since Thursday, two days before she was discovered, had been received from the distressed vessel.

Two smashed dories and an empty life raft indicated the crew had not lasted long in the freezing waters once they launched the dories to escape the grounded wreck. There were no survivors. On charter to Eastern Fisheries of Souris, PEI, *Iceland II* carried ten men: Captain Thomas Hodder, aged 31, and Reginald Foote both hailed from Burin, Newfoundland; mate Leslie MacDonald, chief engineer Albert MacDonald 21, James Carter 23, Clarence Malone 25, Lee Jenkins 30, David O'Hanley and John Hendsbee, 38, all of Souris, PEI; and Clovis Gallant, 35, Rustico, PEI.

By Saturday, February 25, 1967, when the storm abated, the toll of the sea was one of the worst in the history of the Atlantic seaboard — four ships with thirty-five men lost in three of them: *Cape Bonnie* lost on February 21 with her crew of eighteen; *Polly and Robbie* on February 21-23 with seven men; *Iceland II* grounded between February 22-23 drowning her ten sailors; *Maureen and Michael* went down on February 23 but her crew of eight were rescued.

Jean Francis (above), a 135-foot schooner built in 1949 by Smith & Rhuland, sank south of Halifax on June 21, 1969. (Photo by C.F. McBride and courtesy of Captain Hubert Hall, Shipsearch Marine, Yarmouth)

Chapter 14 (1967–92)
The fear of oily waters

Shipwrecks around the coast of Nova Scotia, even considering modern advances in technology and communication, are not a thing of the past. Humans, being inventive creatures, will devise and design aids to overcome problems; yet, despite every precaution that can be taken in designing navigational aids, human error and mechanical breakdown can still result in marine disasters. The age-old antagonists — severe weather and rocky shores — still claim ships and lives.

At the mercy of wind, rock and sea

By April 29, 1967, it was all over for another victim on Nova Scotian shores. While her crew slept in Halifax hotels and her skipper kept watch from the cliffs above, the 4,100-ton *Costarican Trader* was being relentlessly pounded against the rocks at Halibut Bay on the western side of the entrance to Halifax harbour.

Grounded early the previous day in towering seas whipped by gales of fifty knots and capped by a blinding snowstorm, *Costarican Trader* was beyond the help of waiting tugs. The 73-foot vessel, registered in Monrovia, Liberia, was headed for Walton, Nova Scotia, in the Minas Basin to take on cargo when she grounded.

Costarican Trader had had rudder troubles the week previous; she had been towed to New Brunswick for repairs and the 73-foot long vessel proceeded on her business into and out of Nova Scotia ports. Built in 1944 and carrying a Greek crew, the freighter ran into trouble after the Halifax harbour pilot left her at 6:15 a.m. April 28, 1967. The pilot left the ship at Mars Rock, about a mile-and-three-quarters from where she went aground. The steering problems that had affected *Costarican Trader* the week before now had her at the mercy of high winds and eventually the unforgiving rocks.

Her first distress call went out about an hour after the pilot left. By mid-day the tugs *Foundation Vigilant* and *Foundation Valiant* surveyed the ship, now lying parallel to the shore about ten yards from a granite cliff. Royal Canadian Navy helicopters lowered tow lines but they broke when the tugs tried to free the rock-bound ship. The storm forced would-be salvagers and rescuers back to Halifax later in the evening.

The crew rescued themselves carrying personal belongings with them. One crewman described *Costarican Trader*, empty of ballast and very light, as "bobbing like a cork" in the violent gale. But it was the same lightness that had put the freighter so far in on the rocks, the crew lowered a gangplank and scampered to safety.

Today the stern section lies on the wreckage-strewn rocks in the shallow water and can be seen even at high tide a few metres north of Halibut Bay. The bow is under water. *Costarican Trader* equipped with modern navigation aids became a victim of wind, rock, and sea.

Arrow near Arichat

Consider the fate of the 11,000-ton, Greek-owned, Liberian-registered oil tanker *Arrow*: on February 4, 1970, while approaching the entrance to the Strait of Canso, she struck Cerberus Rock and grounded solidly.

By the next morning, news of how the wreck occurred was overshadowed by the fear of the 16,000 tons of Bunker C oil spilling into the ocean in Chedabucto Bay. On the evening of February 5, a massive effort involving oil clean-up experts, biologists, and salvage teams began the fight to save the shores of the bay from an ecological catastrophe. Two

Arrow (left) aground on Cerberus Rock, Chedabucto Bay, in early February 1970. Cerberus Rock was perhaps a fitting place for *Arrow* to die — it's named after the three-headed dog with a mane and tail of snakes which guards the entrance to Hades in Greek mythology. (Photo courtesy Captain Hubert Hall, Shipsearch Marine, Yarmouth)

tugs had lines on *Arrow* when she broke apart at the stern. It was hoped the stern section would float away, but deck and hull plates held the piece closeby.

The forward section, with nineteen of the ship's twenty-seven oil compartments, remained on Cerberus Rock, about four miles from Arichat, oozing congealed bunker fuel into the bay. Soon a five-mile section of the coast line from Arichat to the tip of Cape Auget was coated with oil, which in places collected in thick black pools. Fox Island Beach, eighteen miles from Canso, reported oil pollution and dead sea birds.

The Canadian Minister of Transportation, Don Jamieson, ordered the ship and her cargo destroyed, but officials at the scene knew that to burn or contain the oil or to sink the hulk was virtually impossible. One week after *Arrow* grounded, the stern section sank in about 100 feet of water. Priority shifted from salvaging the remaining oil from the hulk to containing pollution. Large oil patches drifted to shore on the Cape Breton side of Chedabucto Bay, but oil was less widespread on the Nova Scotia mainland side. On February 12, as a world-wide appeal went out for anti-pollution material and expertise, only the antenna masts of *Arrow's* forward section were visible. *Arrow* settled lower in the water each day. The resultant pressure squeezed new oil from the sunken wreck.

Today, the remains of *Arrow* lie under water awaiting final destruction with no mercy from wind and wave. The bow section lies at the base of Cerberus Rock, scattered, twisted and intertwined with wrecks of older vintage. The stern hulk is virtually intact and is often visited by scuba divers who like to explore the tanker's remains and to take photos. Viewing these bones of 1970 gives visible proof that man's ingenuity and technology often takes second place to the rocky shores of Nova Scotia.

Carita (above), formerly named *Ingrid Gorthon*, blew ashore at Money Point, near Cape Smokey on the northern tip of Cape Breton Island on December 20, 1976. A power failure put her at the mercy of the seas. (Photo courtesy Captain Hubert Hall, Shipsearch Marine, Yarmouth)

Old shipwreck, modern view

In 1840 George Old emigrated from Dorset, England, to Trinity Bay, Newfoundland, where he met and married Mary Newhook. Old and his bride didn't stay in Newfoundland long, but moved to Boularderie Island, Bras d'Or Lake, Nova Scotia.

George Old was a shipwright by trade and while residing at Boularderie Island he built several vessels, including a 600-ton barque in 1848 which he christened *Inconstant*. The ship, owned by T.D. Archibald and her master Robert Coles, was fitted with a half-form female figurehead. The next year this vessel, presumably under Coles, sailed to the British Isles where it had a contract to carry cargo to Peru. Rather than take the treacherous Cape Horn crossing, he sailed east via the Cape of Good Hope across the Indian Ocean.

One stop on the long route was Wellington, New Zealand. But upon entering Wellington harbour, *Inconstant* struck a rock punching a hole in her side. *Inconstant* sank and the point where she grounded is still known as Inconstant Point. A survey tug towed the hulk to Lambton Quay in Wellington.

After several months she was put up for sale and John Plimmer bought the hulk for £80 and beached her near the site of what later became the Bank of New Zealand, Number One. *Inconstant* made a useful wharf for small ships and Plimmer built a large warehouse on her deck. To the amused public, the whole structure had the general appearance of an ark and it wasn't long before she became a Wellington landmark known as "Plimmer's Ark" or "Noah's Ark." By the 1890s it had become obscured by other structures and was partly buried in mud.

The Bank of New Zealand's head office was built on the site in 1899. In 1998 a new head office opened and the old site lay empty. The construction workers of Wellington were preparing the area for the erection of a shopping mall when, in the course of excavation, they came upon the hull of *Inconstant*. Two chairs were made from some pieces, one of which rests in the Turnbull Library and the other in New Zealand's National Museum.

Today, the mall lies over the hull of the old ship. Instead of removing the hull, architects and designers decided to leave it there and to build the mall over the old ship. A section of floor is glass, to allow people to look through the floor and view the bow section of the hull of *Inconstant* — a schooner built by Nova Scotian George Old who married Mary Newhook of Trinity Bay.

The Newhook surname is well established in Trinity Bay, Newfoundland; however, the surname Old is rare in Nova Scotia, for the descendants of George Old moved west and settled mainly in Manitoba. George and Mary Old's gravestones still stand in the Presbyterian Cemetery, Boularderie Island, Nova Scotia.

End of an era

The waters around Nova Scotia are quieter today. Modern equipment, rescue units, lighthouses, and navigation aids have greatly reduced wrecks, marine disasters, and the toll of human lives. No more do we see from high headlands and in the towns, the little vessels that plied the briny ocean.

"The old order changeth, yielding place to new," is certainly applicable to the sea lanes off Nova Scotia. Super highways and roads hastened the end of coasting vessels — those small schooners, like *Wally G*, rushing from port to port delivering food and supplies and trying to safely negotiate Canso Strait. Gone are ships like *Wanita* leaving in the fall for PEI potatoes, battling wind and fog the entire voyage.

Terns like *Reliance*, that once sailed the treacherous Atlantic on overseas trade missions full of dried cod or salt, are gone. The day of the tern schooner came and went almost within a decade or so, but roster books and shipping lists are full of names like *Dorin*, "Lost at sea with crew."

The coal trade dwindled almost to a standstill; thus the colliers, like *Renwick*, once wrecked, were not replaced. Gone are the days when ships like S.S. *Morien* which in 1912 while laden with coal left Nova Scotia and disappeared with seventeen local men, never to be seen again.

As long as Nova Scotian men sailed the sea, the women stayed at home and waited for news of a safe return. Theirs was a world of anxiety, care and waiting. Often the supplication of distressed mariners came to mind: "O' Lord thy sea is so great and my boat is so small." They prayed their menfolk would pass Thrum Cap and Sambro Ledges safely, would escape the dangerous Cerberus Rock or Gannet Shoal, and would sail through Scaterie Passage without incident.

In the new order, the descendants of seafaring pioneers of historic Nova Scotian ports from beautiful Yarmouth harbour, renown Lunenburg and Shelburne, and the bustling narrows of Halifax and Sydney, can only read about and dream of the days of sail that are no more.

Fermont on Seal Island — A view of a modern shipwreck with *Fermont* fatally aground at Seal Island, Nova Scotia in September 1992. (Photo courtesy Captain Hubert Hall, Shipsearch Marine, Yarmouth)

Appendices

Appendix A

On April 21, 1943, the convoy vessel *Fanad Head* collided with the Lunenburg banker *Flora Alberta* about ninety miles east of Sambro Lightship off Nova Scotia.

Eight of *Flora Alberta*'s crew survived: Captain Guy Tanner, Lunenburg; John Knickle, Blue Rocks; Douglas Reinhardt, Garth Reinhardt, John Reinhardt, all of Vogler's Cove; Walter Corkum, Pleasantville; and William Grandy of Garnish, Newfoundland.

Twenty-one men lost their lives:

James Buffett, Lunenburg	Fred Tanner, Blue Rocks
Brantford Ritcey, Rose Bay	Stanley Tanner, Blue Rocks
Ronald Miller, Blue Rocks	Bertie Tanner, Blue Rocks
Fred Morash, Blue Rocks	Eldridge Richardson, Blue Rocks
Ira Smith, Vogler's Cove	Wesley Anderson, Dayspring
James Malloy, Lunenburg	Samuel Mills, Lunenburg (born in NF)
Clifford Selig, Lunenburg	Gordon Levy, Lunenburg
Charles Walsh, North West	Charles Ernst, East LaHave
Lawrence Ernst, East LaHave	Nicholas Antle, Burin, NF
Michael Smith, Burin, NF	Edgar Mahar, Sr., Harbour Breton, NF
Henry Best, Lunenburg (born in Merasheen, NF)	

Appendix B

Some citizens of Upper and Lower Prospect and Terence Bay involved in rescue of survivors of the liner *Atlantic* in 1873:

Mr. Clancy	Mr. Kerr (Customs)	Magistrate Ryan	Mr. Marckwald
Squire Ryan	William Sillick	John P. Christian	Samuel White
Samuel Christian	Patrick Christian	Patrick Duggan	James Power
John Duggan	John Purcell	Michael Purcell	Martin Marlin
Joseph Slaunwhite	Rev. G.M. Grant, St. Matthew's Church		

George J. Longard, Justice of the Peace, Upper Prospect
Edmund Ryan, Justice of the Peace, and wife Martha, Lower Prospect
Rev. W.J. Ancient, Anglican clergy, Terence Bay

Within a week, 200 or 300 vessels, mostly Nova Scotian but also from America, visited the wreck scene. Two were named: *Hoover* from Halifax and tug *Goliath*, chartered by Customs.

Appendix C

Nova Scotian seamen lost on *Maggie and May*, August 1908:

Capt. Erick McCathran, Gloucester, Massachusetts

Rubon (Reuben?) Porter, Eel Brook

Koch Wentzel, Lunenburg

Delon Porter, Eel Brook

Patrick English, Conception Bay, NF

Walter Fiander, Codroy, NF

Thomas Muse, Eel Brook

Alfred Muse, Eel Brook

Guste Ludeger, Eel Brook

Appendix D

Crew of *Muriel*, a banker owned in the United States but manned by Nova Scotian fishermen. She was sunk by a German U-boat on August 5, 1918; her crew escaped and rowed into Yarmouth.

Captain Eldridge Nickerson, Shag Harbour

Joseph Crowell, Lower Wood's Harbour

Nathaniel Nickerson, Wood's Harbour

Calvin Nickerson, Wood's Harbour

Isaiah D'Entremont, West Pubnico

Willard Larkin, East Pubnico

John L. Brown, West Barraro

Albert Murree, Eel Brook

Jacob Abbott, Argyle

Connell Goodwin, Lower Argyle

William J. Butler, Liverpool

Moses Nickerson, Upper Wood's Harbour

Amos Forbes, Wood's Harbour

Augustus Nickerson, Wood's Harbour

James Belliveau, Wood's Harbour

Jeremiah D'Entremont, West Pubnico

James Gardner, Pubnico Head

Bernard Potter, Belleville

Alton Smith, Atwood's Brook

Gordon Hamilton, Argyle

William Muise, Surrette's Island

Howard Chapman, Port Clyde

Appendix E

Nova Scotian seamen lost on *Rose Castle*: S.S. *Rose Castle* was anchored near Bell Island, Newfoundland, on November 2, 1942 when she was struck by an enemy torpedo. Twenty-eight crewmen lost their lives including fourteen from Nova Scotia:

R. Bennett, Able Bodied Seaman, Newport

A. Bagnell, fireman, Kennington Cove

A. Burke, fireman, Sydney

A.A. Driscoll, Ordinary Seaman, Glace Bay

J. Greene, 3rd mate, Sydney

W. Dwyer, trimmer, Sydney Forks

A. McLeod, oiler, New Boston

A. Gabriel, trimmer, Sydney Forks

J. Myles, bosun, Sydney North

P. McMullen, 4th engineer, Louisbourg

L. Wasson, Able Bodied Seaman, Sydney

M. Matheson, fireman, Big Harbour

W.J. MacDonald, master, Sydney

A.J. Vatcher, 1st mate, Halifax

Town and Vessel Index